More Curiosities of British Children's TV

BEN RICKETTS

CONTENTS

INTRODUCTION

You'll be pleased to know that, once again, I've been delving through the archives to explore the history of British children's TV. And, as per before, I won't be looking at the usual suspects. Instead, I've concentrated on the lesser known and lesser discussed programmes. After all, they're part of our cultural heritage; it would be a mistake to let them slide into complete obscurity. The programmes featured may not be landmark slices of television, but they deserve to have their story told and preserved.

And, for myself, writing this book has been an absorbing journey. The most important part of compiling this book has been tracking down the actual programmes. Without this footage there would be no book. My main port of call is always the BFI Archive, but occasionally I have had to look elsewhere. And this is why I've spent several hours skipping through old VHS tapes which contain home recordings of specific shows. I even found myself, in one instance, being passed footage sourced from a Betamax recording made in Dubai.

However, the most exciting part of the whole research process has been tracking down the people involved in making these shows. Blessed with fantastic memories that defy the decades, these individuals have helped to make this book what it is. Their insights have been invaluable in uncovering the true stories behind the shows. And, for any scholar of British television, you can rest assured that you will find plenty of interest in here.

I've tried to cover as many oddities as I can this time round, so it's unlikely that you will have heard of every programme featured. But hopefully these more obscure shows will pique your curiosity at the very least. I would, ideally, have featured more shows from the 1960s, but sadly the majority of this era is missing from the archives. However, I've upped the 1970s content and also covered several regional oddities. So, once again, enjoy!

IZEENA

ITV
1966

British childhood wouldn't be the same without the wonder of British wildlife. After all, who didn't coo at the beauty of a butterfly, stare in disbelief at the pointed nose of a shrew or rejoice when a hedgehog shuffled into the garden? However, what children yearn for is the unusual. And that's why exotic animals such as monkeys, parrots and chameleons hold such an allure. If you're lucky, you may spy some of these at a zoo or, if you're really lucky, you could be surrounded by them like *Izeena*.

Rumoured to be 200 years old, although each passing day sees her getting younger, Izeena (Fenella Fielding) lives in a treehouse in Animal Land. Against the grass, trees and wide blue skies of Animal Land, Izeena lives a carefree existence where there's no need to take notice of time. Without the daily grind of having to get up and make Dad's breakfast or running to catch the bus, Izeena can concentrate on singing songs about hippos and taking advice from ostriches on stretching exercises.

Peering out of her treehouse, which is flanked by giant flowers, Izeena takes a closer look at the lives of her neighbours in Animal Land. As the real life footage of wildlife plays out, Izeena and the viewers are treated to a series of narrated adventures. Whiskers Warthog has ambitions of being a gazelle and invests significant time in imitating their habits. Romantic strife is never far away with Charlie and Charlotte Chimpanzee falling out over the purchase of a fur coat. And

4

there's even interspecies tension as demonstrated by Bomber Bird's bullying of Hero the Hippo.

An Anglia Television production, *Izeena* consisted of 15 episodes that were 10-minutes each and transmitted on Sunday teatimes at around 5.45pm. But, rather than being a programme that was transmitted nationwide, *Izeena* was only available in the Anglia and Grampian regions. Sadly, due to television programmes being viewed as ephemeral at the time, only two episodes of *Izeena* remain in the archives.

Luckily, these two remaining episodes allow us to get a flavour for what Anglia was cooking up on Sundays. The dubbed animal footage is nothing new; *Animal Magic,* then in its infancy, had been pulling similar tricks over on BBC1 for several years by the time *Izeena* aired. Nonetheless, these sections, with scripts written by Robert Gould and Michael Edwards, are serviceable enough. They may fail to fully engage the viewer, but they're saved by their brief nature.

Much more exciting, and this comes as no surprise, is Fenella Fielding's performance. Fielding's most defining role as the sultry and seductive Valeria in Carry On Screaming would come several months later, but it's clear that this enchanting character was part of Fielding's own DNA. Blessed with a luxurious voice that combines coquettishness with supreme confidence, Fielding engages like few others. And certain sections of *Izeena* are blatantly there to ensure that any watching fathers don't change the channel.

But Fielding's charm is more than just flirtatious gimmickry. It's a trait which is infused with a universal affability. So, whilst the mere thought of someone mimicking the movements of a chameleon may fail to inspire much interest, in the hands of

5

Fielding it becomes an absolute joy. Naturally, it's difficult to judge the series due to the limited material that survives, but the two remaining episodes are evidence it deserved a wider audience. Sure, it may, at times, find itself plodding along, but when Fenella Fielding glides onto the screen, *Izeena* hits the bullseye.

DIANE'S MAGIC THEATRE

ITV
1969 – 1970

Entertainment, thanks to technology, continues to evolve in new and exciting ways. This is why children can now choose from dozens of TV channels dedicated to children's programming. And when it comes to online channels, well, it would take a lifetime to count them all. But performing to children is not the sole preserve of these digital arenas. And you should never underestimate the power of the theatre.

Undeterred by changing fashions, the theatre has maintained a magnetic pull for hundreds of years. The excitement as the curtain rises is unparalleled and, for a child, watching real life performers in three dimensions is a magical experience. But it's not always easy to get to a theatre. Thankfully, television has a solution to this predicament. So, let's grab a ticket and head over to *Diane's Magic Theatre*.

Down at the City Varieties theatre it's showtime. There will be singing, there will be dancing and there will be laughter. Watching this spectacle is Diane (Diane Mewse), but she's not alone in her theatre box. Diane is joined by two rabbits by the names of Bubble and Squeak. And it's these two bunnies who will help dictate the action unfolding on the stage. Taking turns, Bubble and Squeak whisper their request for a particular performance into Diane's ear. These requests, powered by theatrical magic, then manifest themselves on stage.

Taking to the stage are a procession of marionettes that can sing, dance and perform like no other. There's Milly the Poodle singing Mairzy Doats against a Paris backdrop. Jonty the Juggler enters the stage atop a unicycle before showing off his juggling skills. And the blue-suited Cliff Cat entertains the audience with his rendition of There Was a Young Lady from Ealing. The show comes to an end when, in true theatre tradition, the final curtain falls.

A Yorkshire Television production, *Diane's Magic Theatre* ran for just one series of 24 episodes. The fifteen-minute episodes were subject to regional variations, so it's difficult to give definitive transmission details. Jess Yates, long term employee of Yorkshire, produced the series and had previously worked with *Diane Mewse* on *Diane's Magic Book* in 1968.

Roger Stevenson provided the marionettes for *Diane's Magic Theatre* and fondly recalls how he got involved:

"Jess Yates was in charge of children's programmes for Yorkshire in the 1960s and 70s. Jess was a very nice guy, I worked very well with him. He came across me when I was working in the Butlins sites in about 1968/69. He looked at the stuff I was doing and said it was perfect for colour television. Jess already had the name and idea for Diane's Magic Theatre. And he'd built the set in the City Varieties theatre. All I was to do was supply inserts for what went on in the theatre. I believe the recording was continuous, so the sections on stage would be filmed and then they would switch to Diane in her box"

Tradition is at the heart of the theatre and it's also at the heart of *Diane's Magic Theatre*. The grand structures of the City Varieties theatre hark back to a bygone era and instantly summon up the excitement of live entertainment. This traditional theme is bolstered further by the presence of Diane.

8

A well-spoken young lady, Diane is forever dressed in her Sunday best and maintains enthusiasm for the performances. It's a wholesome brand of charm and one that feels archaic when held up to the harsh glare of the 21st century.

Continuing this charm offensive are Roger Stevenson's puppets. And, being an early foray into the world of colour television, these puppets are the perfect participants. Designed with nuanced idiosyncrasies, these puppets appear to feature every single colour in the spectrum. Superb as these visual aesthetics are, it's the prowess behind the performances which is most eye catching.

The puppets all make their way on stage with a bouncy enthusiasm, but there's an intricacy at play which is breathtaking. Certain performances, such as those featuring trapeze acts and jugglers, genuinely appear to defy the laws of physics. But Stevenson confirms that these were all performed by a single set of hands. And this makes the performances all the more remarkable.

These displays are not just limited to the stage. Diane, of course, is joined in her grand box by a pair of glove puppets in the guise of Bubble and Squeak. These sections provide a quick break from the action on stage and foster a sense of variety. And thanks to Stevenson's talents (again), Bubble and Squeak feel just as conscious and sentient as Diane. The trio's chemistry has a strong vibrancy and their repartee helps each section to segue smoothly.

A superb showcase for the wonders of colour television, *Diane's Magic Theatre* is good natured fun. It's certainly not as well-known as other puppet series of the era, but it provides a welcome alternative to the world of Gerry Anderson. The series succeeds in capturing the excitement of live performances and does it in a manner which is both endearing and eye catching. Long may the theatre reign.

EDANDZED!

BBC1
1970

Robots, despite their rigid and emotionless personalities, are ubiquitous entities on our television screens. But enough about reality TV stars. Sorry, that was below the belt. But true. Anyway, your traditional nuts, bolts and PCB robots have *also* carved out nice careers on television. One of the earliest to be gifted their own show, however, is rarely acknowledged by the history books. His human co-star, though, is a much firmer fixture. And, together, *EdandZed!* helped to push forward the evolution of Saturday morning television.

Ed 'Stewpot' Stewart is the host of *EdandZed!* and, judging by the opening titles, he makes his way to the studio straight from his Radio 1 show *Junior Choice*. Racing through the streets on his bicycle is treacherous enough, but what will he find at Television Centre? Well, he'll find Zed. Designed to eliminate technical faults, Zed is a robot who believes that he's the star. And it's here that a battle for supremacy is established. Zed, with his strong Brummie accent, is convinced that the show should be renamed ZedandEd! but Ed is having none of it.

EdandZed! is, to the relief of the viewers, about much more than human/robot bickering. Its main thrust is entertainment. And it gets off to a good start by embracing pop music. Rolling into the studio are a procession of bands that include White Plains, Mud, Hot Chocolate and Herman's Hermits. It's down to these groups to open and close each episode with a song, but there's much more in between.

To start with, there are mini sketches shot on location such as cowboy Ed chasing a bandit to the strains of Ride Your Pony. And, to add some filmic glamour, Ed's Electric Kinema serves up clips from Fantasia and The Wizard of Oz. Finally, each week features the illustrated adventures of Ed the Eminent Expert, a crime solving genius.

The man responsible for bringing *EdandZed!* to our screens was Paul Ciani. No stranger to Saturday morning children's television, Ciani had previously devised and directed *Zokko!* between 1968 – 1970. *EdandZed!* ran in the same timeslot as *Zokko!* but, with only nine episodes to its name, *EdandZed!* was noticeably shorter. Thankfully, the infamous purges of the BBC archives were relatively kind to *EdandZed!* with only two episodes known to be missing.

Central to the series are, as the title suggests Ed and Zed. And with regular stints on *Top of the Pops, Crackerjack* and the radio, Ed Stewart was a much loved broadcaster. *EdandZed!* cashes in on his engaging appeal by putting him centre stage. Stewart's cheery confidence is well suited to a young audience and it's only magnified when he's paired up with Zed.

Sure, Zed's visual aesthetics (including egg whisk antennae) would rule him out of even the most budget stricken episode of *Doctor Who*, but his friendly design is enough to entertain children. And, together, Ed and Zed provide a wonderful clash of egos as they battle for control; Ed gets Zed dumped in the BBC bins whilst Zed locks Ed in his dressing room just before a show.

To a cultural historian, or indeed any music fan, the bands featured on *EdandZed!* provide the most interesting aspect of the series. The bands aren't exactly what you would class as mega bands of the era, but they are a nice indicator of the post-60s landscape. Mud, attired in deafening dungarees, pop up to perform Jumping Jehosaphat. White Plains are in the studio to knock out My Baby Loves Lovin. And Herman's Hermits serve up the hits. Okay, the performances are mimed, but this doesn't seem to bother the audience members bopping away.

Music, however, is but one string to the bow of *EdandZed!* Variety is the order of the day and this is what the series delivers. The Electric Kinema section brings a dash of Hollywood to proceedings. Ed the Eminent Expert, featuring mysteries such as a missing diamond ring and the secret ingredient of French perfume being stolen, grants the series a narrative flavour. And the comedy offered by Zed – an endless stream of malapropisms – is just perfect for the budding comedy receptors of children.

EdandZed! may share a similar template to *Zokko!* but it's more recognisable as Saturday morning children's TV. Whereas *Zokko!* had no sentient presence on presenter duties, *EdandZed!* has at least one in Ed Stewart. Likewise, the presence of a studio audience hints at the participatory nature of shows to come. Paul Ciani would have one more go at honing his formula of Saturday morning programming in 1973 with *Outa-Space,* but the following year saw the birth of *Tiswas.* And things were never the same again.

GRASSHOPPER ISLAND

ITV
1971

There are two schools of thought when it comes to the merits of being stranded on a desert island. One is that it almost guarantees certain death due to a combination of thirst, hunger and heatstroke. The second is that it's a nonstop barrel of fun involving hammocks, coconuts and buried treasure.

For a child, the latter vision is preferable and confirms this as the go-to choice for any island fantasy. But for some children it need not remain a fantasy. The daily grind of the city can soon be swapped for island life. However, on *Grasshopper Island*, instead of coconuts, you're more likely to be getting to grips with, well, grasshoppers.

Living in a tall house with plenty of room to run up and down, but never sideways, three brothers are planning a great escape. Smarty (Max Whitby), who has answers for all the questions, is joined by his aspiring soldier of a brother Toughy (Tim Whitby) and Mouse (Nick Whitby), their cheese loving sibling. Fed up with being looked after by a succession of carers, collectively known as The Voices of Authority (Tim Brooke-Taylor), the brothers decide to run away to sea.

But, hitching a ride on a ship proves problematic for Smarty, Toughy and Mouse as none of the boats are willing to take them on. Thankfully, a route to the high seas is soon opened up when they stumble across the Elderly Boy (Charles Hawtrey) who is quite unlike any sailor they've ever seen before. Not quite old and not quite young, the Elderly Boy is the proud

14

owner of a converted lifeboat and rather keen on finding an uninhabited island. Joining forces, this quartet sets sail and eventually land on a deserted island which they name Grasshopper Island.

The Elderly Boy soon decides that his legs aren't used to life on dry land, so departs whilst Smarty, Toughy and Mouse set up home in an abandoned cottage. But the brothers are not alone. On the other side of the island there lives a most curious couple. An inhabitant on Grasshopper Island for over 20 years, Cornelius Button (Julian Orchard) has dedicated his life to studying grasshoppers and gobbling pungent cheese. The odour of this cheese, however, is one of many sticking points for his domineering housekeeper Lupus (Patricia Hayes), who is exasperated by Cornelius' every action.

After making grasshopper wine, foraging for eggs and digging up a dairy-heavy treasure, the brothers eventually become acquainted with Cornelius and Lupus. Striking up firm friendships, the two camps appear to have settled into a joyful existence. Unfortunately, Cornelius' arch-nemesis, the meddling Dr Hopper (Frank Muir), soon arrives and is determined to take ownership of the island. The only way that Cornelius can keep control of the island is by producing proof of the rare Blue Buttons grasshopper. But it's so rare that he hasn't seen one for 20 years.

An independent production written and produced by Joy Whitby, who had previously created *Play School* and *Jackanory* for the BBC, *Grasshopper Island* was a 12 episode series that first aired on ITV in the Granada region before gradually spreading round the other ITV franchises. Despite the series' success, which would go on to be sold around the world, getting

Grasshopper Island off the ground wasn't easy as Joy Whitby recounts:

"I was one of the six television executives who resigned from London Weekend in 1969 in support of Michael Peacock. Having left the BBC to join the new franchise and now losing my job at LWT, a lot of doors were closed in children's television. I went to Corfu on a family holiday and watching our three small sons playing on the beach, I wondered how they would manage on their own.   When we got home I started writing Grasshopper Island *while deciding what to do next.*

I had planned to shoot Grasshopper Island *in Corfu but the fascist colonels had taken over and the UK unions banned filming in Greece. Frank Muir had also resigned from LWT and we remained firm friends. He suggested I filmed in Corsica where his family had a holiday home. By great good fortune, a friend went to a dinner party where she met a young merchant banker who expressed an interest in financing films. We were introduced and he formed a syndicate to raise the money"*

Slightly easier was the casting which, thanks to previous working relationships, allowed Joy Whitby to piece together a rather stellar cast of actors as she remembers:

"Having been responsible for Jackanory before I left the BBC probably helped when casting. I had admired The Goodies *and their cameraman, Tony Leggo. I suppose the lure of nine weeks in Corsica played its part in securing his expertise. He recommended Tim Brooke-Taylor. I had worked with Patricia Hayes and Julian Orchard who were happy to join the team. I thought Charles Hawtrey would be an ideal Elderly Boy and he must have fancied a change from his* Carry On *films. All the actors were contracted in the usual way through their agents – except for Frank. The*

16

last episode featured a baddy called Dr Hopper. Marty Feldman was to have played him, but at the last moment he had to pull out so Frank stepped in"

Looking back at the nuts and bolts of putting the programme together, Joy Whitby suspects that such a production wouldn't necessarily be successful or fully realised in the modern world of broadcasting:

"I couldn't embark on such a risky venture now. We did so then because with the money in place and such an experienced team, we ignored how disastrous such an enterprise could be. We assumed Family Programmes would take it because it seemed such a classic BBC product. In fact they turned it down. ITV bought it and it has sold all round the world. It is still selling as a DVD.

In those days, it was the norm for any established producer in-house to be trusted without too much interference. Programme ideas only needed to be approved by the head of your department. Money was allocated and your job was to be creative and realise your idea with a lot of in-house support. Today, producers need rubber-stamping from one boss after another before getting the go-ahead, often leading to frustrating compromises along the way"

The image of a group of boys making their way through life on an uninhabited, sun kissed island is straight out of Boy's Own magazine, but *Grasshopper Island* brings a slight twist. For, whilst there are a plethora of traditional island based japes such as fishing, swimming and exploring, this all coincides with a cheerfully absurd edge And that's why the viewer is treated to a torrent of surreal moments such as Mouse tracking down a mythical egg tree and the gleefully ridiculous escapades of Cornelius trying to hide his cheese from Lupus.

This combination of surrealistic antics and the more conventional moments makes for a balanced set of narratives. Although there is a slight story arc present, as the boys come to grips with life on the island, all the episodes work as standalone jaunts. Anyone tuning in, even midway through the series, would have been able to dive in headfirst.

This ease of accessibility, of course, is also down to the characters crafted by Joy Whitby and the cast that bring them to life. The three Whitby brothers make for a fine combination of idiosyncrasies and, by virtue of their familial connections, there's a natural chemistry bubbling away. The adult cast, meanwhile, is a remarkable ensemble and one that hints at the respect reserved for Joy Whitby's creativity.

Tim Brooke-Taylor, Charles Hawtrey and Frank Muir may only feature briefly, but it's a joy to see them all in action, particularly Tim Brooke-Taylor who drags up in the very finest 70s traditions. And Brooke-Taylor retains fond memories of working on the show:

"I was working for Radio 4 at the time. Tony Whitby was the controller and we were very grateful to him for various reasons – not least because he commissioned the first series of 'I'm Sorry I Haven't a Clue' the following year, 1972. The cameraman, Tony Leggo, was someone I'd worked with and Joy, who turned out to be a Goodies fan, got his advice that I was good with hats (an inexpensive way of playing different characters). I loved the filming, especially being bossy and authoritative to the boys. My only regret was not going to the island to film. I worked with Joy quite a few times after that, including voicing a French cartoon series,

Julian Orchard is probably less well known than his co-stars but his comedic flair allows him to transform Cornelius into a bumbling, childlike eccentric with ease. Patricia Hayes, meanwhile, is in her element as the tough, no nonsense housekeep Lupus who, behind the steely exterior, possesses a soft, maternal charm. They make a compelling double act and their chemistry strengthens the series no end.

Underpinning all of this is the unmistakable brilliance of Joy Whitby. Having been the architect behind two shows that continue to act as a blueprint for children's TV over 50 years on, Whitby is well placed to create children's television. And this, in part, is down to her dedication to not only creating strong scripts, but also to succeed without the backing of a major channel. *Grasshopper Island* may not be as well-known as other programmes on Whitby's CV, but it's a personal triumph and fantastic fun for the viewers.

RING-A-DING

BBC1
1973

Parents have been scratching their heads since time immemorial as regards the best methods for keeping their children entertained. Thankfully, there's a recipe for success to achieve this. And it's a simple mixture of singing, playing games and using the imagination. It's likely that our cave dwelling ancestors employed similar techniques to great success, but they weren't half as lucky as us. After all, we've also been able to call upon the brilliance of children's TV and Derek Griffiths. And, if you want to see how potent this combination can be, just take a look at *Ring-a-Ding*.

With a background constructed from a set of giant building blocks, Derek Griffiths finds himself in the world of *Ring-a-Ding*. And it's a world where the emphasis is on fun. Armed with just a guitar and minimal props, Griffiths gives a one man performance that takes in the worlds of rhyme, song and imagination.

One moment, Griffiths can be conjuring up a mother duck and her ducklings with just his hands through the power of mime while, a moment later, he may have grasped his guitar and started belting out a song about happy feet. Likewise, the stories featured are inventive microcosms of literature such as Bert's Boot which features a wellington boot convinced that it's a hat. And, finally, games featured include matching a selection of shoes to the right people and figuring out which animal Griffiths has stealthily removed from a farmyard scene.

Emerging into the unforgiving cold of January 1973, *Ring-a-Ding* ran for 13 episodes as part of the Watch with Mother slot at lunchtimes. Coupled alongside broadcasts of *Teddy Edward*, the 10-minute episodes of *Ring-a-Ding* found themselves airing in Friday's BBC1. Repeats of *Ring-a-Ding* continued for a few years with the show's final transmission coming in 1977. The series was written and directed by Peter Charlton who had previously taken up the same roles on *Play School* and would later work on *Play Away*, *We are the Champions* and *Bitsa*.

Looking back into the early 1970s, Peter Charlton takes up the story of *Ring-a-Ding's* inception:

"My boss at the time, Cynthia Felgate, was asked to produce a new series for the Watch with Mother slot and she asked me to come up with an idea. And Ring-a-Ding was the result. Cynthia was great, very encouraging and very aware. In a way her background was very similar to mine in that we had both started off in children's theatre and she would let you make a mistake every now and then. I originally envisioned Derek in a set of giant building blocks. All we needed was a cyclorama and space; I can't imagine the scenic budget was very big"

The frontman and public face of *Ring-a-Ding*, Derek Griffiths appeared to be on children's television every single day in the 1970s. This made for a hectic schedule and one which involved shifting quickly from one project to the next. Accordingly, Griffiths' memories of *Ring-a-Ding* are a little dusty. Luckily, with a gentle dusting, Griffiths was able to recall the programme with more detail:

"Getting involved with Ring-a-Ding was a fairly simple process: Peter

Charlton asked me and I said yes! As Peter was writing and directing the episodes, this meant he knew exactly what he wanted; this is always important in television and also made for an easy recording process. As I was the only presenter on the series, the main challenge was not to be boring and always be entertaining. The only real difficulty I can remember is having to sit on brightly coloured blocks in tight jeans"

A key feature of children's television is variety and *Ring-a-Ding* comes packed with more variety than a box of Quality Street. From the insanely catchy theme tune with its jaunty, infectious rhymes through to the quirky stories and colourful guessing games, *Ring-a-Ding* is more than capable of going head to head with that most testing challenge: a pre-schooler's attention span.

The set may be designed with economy in mind, but, in truth, there's little need for a lavish set and, as with most things in life, simplicity is the correct path to tread here. The building block background both satisfies the need for bright colours in children's television and allows Derek Griffiths a simple arena to underline his skills as a presenter.

Griffiths is synonymous with children's television and *Ring-a-Ding* helps to strengthen his legacy even more. As a matter of fact, if you were to have never experienced Griffiths in *Play School, Heads and Tails* and *Cabbages and Kings*, then *Ring-a-Ding* would serve as the perfect introduction to his talents. Whether he's tiptoeing a pair of fingers up along his body from his toes to his nose, getting viewers to guess which item of a food is hidden in a photo or, more simply, singing a song about an ugly duckling, Griffiths is in fine form here.

Peter Charlton is keen to sing Griffiths' praises as well as revealing the adversity often faced by actors:

"With Derek you get 3-in-1: he's a very good actor, nice singer and an extremely good musician who can play several instruments. He's very funny and he's one of the best mimes in the business — you don't need much else. And he's really easy to work with. The one problem I remember with Ring-a-Ding was that, as it was going to be repeated for three years, it had to be pretty flawless. And one particular edition, Derek had flu and we had to do about 20 takes of one song. We both knew we had to get it right. There was no option to say we'll take a day off and do it tomorrow. We had to get it right on the day"

Regardless of the restrictions caused by tight jeans and the strength sapping effects of flu, Griffiths remains engaging throughout. And, for a solo presenter, this is the pinnacle of achievement. As a rather sad footnote to the *Ring-a-Ding* story, only five of the thirteen episodes have been retained by the BBC. This situation is due to their decision to junk what was considered less commercial material. It's a regrettable state of affairs, but we should be grateful that these five episodes remain. Although they're not genre-busting examples of television, they *are* a testament to all the talents involved.

RAGTIME

BBC1
1973 – 1975

Childhood blesses us with an almost infinite sense of wonder. And, even in the most mundane objects, there seems to lay a world of possibilities to keep us entertained for hours. And this is a real boon for parents. It is, for example, much cheaper to supply a child with a discarded toilet roll than take them to the zoo.

It's important, though, to disregard the importance of a parent's bank balance in these situations. The real treasure, in a discarded toilet roll, is not budget related. It's more to do with an unparalleled strengthening of the imagination. And, with a collection of spoons, old doilies and socks, *Ragtime* is on hand to take this concept and run with it.

Fronted by Maggie Henderson and Fred Harris, *Ragtime* is a series with one foot firmly entrenched in the world of wordplay and the other tapping and waggling its toes in a landscape of unbridled imagination. Episodes begin with a joyously upbeat ragtime workout on the piano. But it's not played by either Maggie or Fred. It's belted out by a flame haired and nifty fingered rag doll. In fact, in terms of population, humans are severely outnumbered in the *Ragtime* universe as Maggie's green cloth bag reveals.

Within this bag are a selection of intriguing puppets that include Dax the dachshund, the Spoon family, Sniff the Dog and aspiring poet Humbug the tiger. The *Ragtime* studio is also home to the unusual Bubble, a curious cushion whose thoughts are displayed in a bubble. And these puppets, courtesy of Maggie and Fred's stealthy hands, enjoy a peculiar existence.

Sally Spoon desperately longs for an Aunt and, following a speedy courtship, eventually gets one as her Uncle Pasty marries Vanilla the Spoon. Meanwhile, Sniff the dog discusses the various objects that have featured in his dreams. And, despite realising the limitations of being a sock on Fred's hand, Humbug opens up and talks about his dream of becoming a footballer's sock.

Ragtime made up part of the Watch with Mother schedule and consisted of two 13-episode series. The first series aired on Wednesday lunchtimes with the second finding its home on Sunday afternoons. *Ragtime* was devised, written and produced by the one-man powerhouse that was Michael Cole. He was joined, in production, by his wife Joanne who, along with her sister, designed all the puppets.

Ragtime was an early step in Fred Harris' television career and, despite the intervening decades, his memories of joining the programme remain vibrant:

"Late in 1972, I wrote to Play School asking to be considered as a presenter. I didn't hear back for many months (and was thinking I'd wasted a fourpenny stamp!) but then suddenly in about April 1973, I got a letter to come up to London to meet a producer, Michael Cole. What I didn't know was that Michael was looking for a male presenter for a new puppet show which he was devising.

To cut a long story short, I got through the auditions and did two try-out weeks of Play School, one of them directed by Michael. This was his way of (a) getting me used to working in a tv studio, which was totally new to me and (b) seeing whether we could work together/ stand each other. He had me doing character voices and working with a sock puppet, and also doing some mime sequences. As it turned out, we got on really well and he offered me the Ragtime job"

Despite *Ragtime* being an award-winning success, there were no plans for a third series. But this is far from a comment on its quality as Fred Harris reveals:

"The award was the SFTA (Society of Film and Television Arts) Harlequin Award, which was renamed BAFTA a year or two later. On the strength of that, the Beeb made an LP record and a second series of Ragtime, but I don't think there were ever any plans for more. When you're making shows for pre-schoolers, there's a fresh audience coming along every couple of years, so two series (repeated) was enough. After all, that's 26 programmes"

Ragtime was repeated several times up until 1980 before being retired from the schedules and taking up residence in the BBC archive. Sadly, the entire series was not destined to remain there. Many episodes of *Ragtime* were junked during a digital transfer programme in the early 1990s. The logic employed was that, in certain cases, only a small sample of a programme's inventory was required. Putting this rather depressing revelation to one side, you can rest assured that the eight remaining episodes are a joy.

Ragtime has a structure which is instantly recognisable as children's television. Much like *Play School* there are songs, stories and puppets at the heart of *Ragtime*. Yet this is where the similarities end. *Ragtime* is much more absurd. A case in point is the puppets. Whereas Big Ted et al ruled the *Play School* roost

26

from a mute perspective, the puppets of *Ragtime* are more lively and vocal. Their designs, too, are noticeably more surreal with characters such as Bubble and Humbug completely off-kilter.

Ragtime may be packed full of puppets, but it's also about learning. One of the skills most valued by *Ragtime* is the magic of wordplay. And it demonstrates this with a series of games, rhymes and songs that explore language. They're simple affairs, but playful enough to stick in the mind e.g. Bubble's story about an aunt with a plant on a slant.

Visual skills are also a crucial step in terms of development. Being able to identify symbols, for example, is a necessary skill to possess. And *Ragtime* is on hand to serve up child-friendly exercises in this area. Therefore, you can expect to find the viewers being asked to guess various shapes which are being drawn on the screen. Best of all, these drawings come courtesy of an out-of-sight Quentin Blake.

All of this learning is bolstered by the presence of Maggie and Fred. Maggie, whose gorgeous voice soaks the opening theme in brilliance, is a woman for whom engagement is a natural trait. And Fred, a true stalwart of children's television, is on classic form. His kindly brand of charm and wide-eyed innocence is in full flow and it's difficult to imagine television without him.

Together, Maggie and Fred conjure up a joyful chemistry which ensures that even a conversation between two wooden spoons about a hole in a dress is a thing of wonder. Harris is keen to expand on the magic behind this chemistry:

"We did have a great relationship; and I wonder if that's because we had totally different ways of approaching the job. Maggie was extremely

27

polished and careful. She would be word-perfect on the script, and would always find the best way of inflecting a line or giving a look to camera. Vision mixers love that – they know that they can time their cuts and mixes really accurately, just the way it was rehearsed.

I came from a totally different background: I'd been working with a participatory drama company for three years – a lot of what we did was improvised and spontaneous. So, to begin with, I treated the script as a rough and ready road map; I'd just throw myself in and see how it turned out. That was generally okay for Play School, but not on a puppet show, where the timings and cues have to be fairly precise. Over time, I learned a bit of Maggie's precision (not much, I'm afraid) and she started to throw in some off-the-cuff lines. It was good for both of us"

Now, for anyone who has ever watched a show produced by Michael Cole before, and that's probably everyone who picks up this book, you'll be aware of his thoroughbred expertise. Fred Harris agrees and remembers working with a man who was exceptionally talented:

"Michael was a really lovely bloke. He was very passionate about giving children respect, and never underestimating their intelligence. Privately, he was a poet, and was very interested in Zen and Eastern philosophy. On one Ragtime song, Maggie tells the story of the Chinese sage who dreams he is a butterfly. When he wakes up he is confused, wondering "Did I dream I was a butterfly, or is he dreaming now he's me?" A philosophy student could write a lengthy treatise on the questions that raises, but Mike knew it was something a child could think about too.

He loved exploring the sense of wonder of a child discovering the world. But he also had a wacky side to him: he loved wordplay, and would make *up silly nonsense songs for spoon characters like Uncle Casserole or Humbug. Sometimes he would have a zany, upbeat item followed immediately by something sensitive and lyrical. His skill was in making that transition work"*

Michael Cole's talents in crafting winsome slices of children's TV have rarely been matched and *Ragtime* is a fine example of his art. Yes, despite the BAFTA win and a cult status amongst those of a certain age, *Ragtime* is barely mentioned in the grand history of children's television. Nonetheless, here is a show that hits a succession of highs and is joyously entertaining along the way.

THE SMALL WORLD OF SAMUEL TWEET

BBC1
1974 – 1975

The presence of a lisp in an individual tends to generate nothing less than a lifetime of ridicule. But a lisp should never be taken as an indicator of buffoonery. Winston Churchill had a lisp and it didn't stop him achieving a thing or two. If one man with a lisp can fight a continental battle against fascism then, surely, running a pet shop should offer few obstacles.

Sadly, even a mundane setting such as a pet shop can prove problematic to someone with a lisp. It doesn't help, of course, if said individual makes a point of conforming to the stereotype of a lisping buffoon. And that's why a cavalcade of chaos is never far away in *The Small World of Samuel Tweet*.

Samuel Tweet (Freddie Davies) is the proprietor of the only pet shop in Chumpton Green. A small, olde worlde town, Chumpton Green falls under the preserve of the eponymous Lord Chumpton (Cardew Robinson). Tweet is a well-meaning chap, yet he has a clumsiness which is unparalleled in Chumpton Green. If something has been carefully stacked then you can rest assured that Tweet will tumble head first into it. And this is in sharp contrast to the organisation that Lord Chumpton is looking to infuse Chumpton Green with.

Despite these differing outlooks on life, Tweet and Lord Chumpton maintain a civil relationship. Lord Chumpton's highly strung nephew, Russell Chumpton (Norman Turkington), however, cannot tolerate a single second of Tweet's. But Tweet isn't on his own when it comes to facing the trials of life in Chumpton Green. For one thing, he always has his trusty Homburg hat to protect him from the exasperation of Russell. There's also the option for Tweet to call upon jovial policeman PC Wicketts (Colin Edwynn) and the kindly Miss Doogoodie (Damaris Hayman) for help.

And Tweet frequently needs help. Setting up a safari park for Lord Chumpton, entering the local elections and dealing with Auntie Ada isn't easy. But these are the ordeals awaiting Tweet. And this is all without mentioning the mysterious 'thing' which lurks within a hamper in the pet shop and communicates in a sequence of aggressive growls.

It was in 1964 that Freddie Davies first came to the attention of British television viewers with an appearance on *Opportunity Knocks*. Following this performance, which led to him being dubbed Freddie 'Parrot Face' Davies, there were further appearances on shows including *The Good Old Days*, *Billy Cotton's Music Hall* and *The Val Doonican Show*. And it was towards the end of the 1960s, as Davies remembers, that *The Small World of Samuel Tweet* started to take shape:

"Gary Knight was my writer from 1967, he had a partnership with Wally Malston who went on to work with Bob Monkhouse. Gary had written a ten minute sketch in 1969 with Samuel Tweet as a pet shop owner and it was shelved. A few years later, Tony Harrison was producing The Coal Hole Club with The Grumbleweeds and I guested on one episode. Tony asked me if I had had any thoughts on a children's TV series so... out came the sketch! We developed it into 25 minutes and did a black and white pilot with an audience of kids"

The series was produced by BBC Manchester with filming

taking place at the Dickinson Road studios, a converted church which was also *Top of the Pop's* first home. The opening sequence, featuring Tweet being followed Pied Piper style by a string of children, was filmed just outside Blackpool in the picturesque village of Wrea Green. These opening titles, accompanied by theme tune The Ballad of Samuel Tweet, helped to announce each of the 12 episodes which were spread over two series.

The Small World of Samuel Tweet is a show which has appeared to work hard at being forgotten. Many episodes were, for a considerable amount of time, missing from the BBC's archives and it was only down to the efforts of an early adopter of home recording that the majority of these were returned. Somebody at the BBC was clearly a fan, hence the second series, but due to a lack of repeats the show has wriggled away from the memories of most. But it's not without merit.

With farce at the very heart of its narratives, *Samuel Tweet* could easily be seen as a Frank Spencer for the under-10s. Freddie Davies takes to slapstick well and can crash into stacked tins with the very best of them. He's not one to shy away from a stunt either; one episode sees him being hoisted up high on a rope to rescue a cat. Talking of animals, there's one scene in the very final episode where an elephant – yes, an actual elephant from Robert Brothers circus – invades the set and smashes it up. So there's lots of chaos.

The pandemonium caused by Tweet's endeavours creates a nice dichotomy with the idealised portrait of life in Chumpton Green. It's a very English way of living and one that has generated lots of gentle comedy over the years. And *Samuel Tweet* uses this patchwork quilt of caddish Lords and bobbies on the beat to give the show its comic identity.

However, it's a brand of comedy which struggles to lift its head above the parapet of hilarity. Too often it feels underbaked and strangely static. Certain sections cry out for a live studio audience to enhance the comedy while other segments are overlong. A further run through the edit suite is required, but time, as ever, is money. Nonetheless, there are still comic highlights. The chemistry between Tweet and PC Wicketts – particularly their impressions routine in the Gala Opening episode – is one of the most enjoyable aspects.

And the second series ups its game with the introduction of Russell Chumpton, a man steeped in perennial anger who provides the necessary conflict to ratchet up the comedy. Despite these nuggets of comic joy, the laugh rate doesn't hit the heights of more successful comedy shows for children. It's this aspect of *Samuel Tweet* which proves to be its Achilles heel in becoming more than a vague footnote of television.

For Freddie Davies the programme proved to be somewhat of a frustrating affair, the effect of which was amplified by the economies of making television:

"It ran two series but I felt it really wasn't what I imagined the character of Samuel Tweet doing – when I first conceived him he was an arrogant idiot who kept complaining about duff budgies. He did move to other things as we ran out of ideas for budgies. But I was never allowed or invited to try other characters which I feel I could have done. All the producers wanted was the hat thing! And TV comedy in the seventies, particularly children's TV comedy, had very small budgets. Samuel Tweet had to be done as live and no editing time was allotted. One episode we did live owing to some strike or other. If I had my time over again, and given

33

the same situation, I would not do it. It was, as I say, of its day!"

Samuel Tweet doesn't position itself as a defining moment of children's TV, yet it's far from a disaster. The performances throughout are superb and there's an undeniable charm about the lisping, bumbling Tweet. The character was strong enough, given the right vehicle, to lead the children of Britain on a merry dance, but *Samuel Tweet* falls just short of this goal.

THE LAUGHING POLICEMAN

ITV
1974 – 1976

There's a tendency for our pulse to rise exponentially and our palms to become drenched in sweat at the mere sight of a policeman. After all, we all commit some form of low level crime every day. Maybe it's creeping marginally over the speed limit. Maybe it's pinching a sweet from the Pick 'n' Mix display. And, in extreme cases, it's watching reality TV. As children, though, policemen radiate nothing but a sense of security, justice and the skill to help an elderly lady across the road. And, if you run across *The Laughing Policeman*, he might even treat you to a few rhymes and songs.

A proud member of his local constabulary, PC254 (Deryck Guyler) regularly finds himself on the beat and outside R. Peels Television and Repairs Shop. Rather than containing an array of dusty, malfunctioning television sets, however, it houses a whole procession of singing, dancing animal puppets. This rather curious collection of green cats, flamingos and teddy bears belt out such pop classics as Yummy Yummy Yummy, One of Those Songs and Daughter of Darkness. These performances are all watched through the shop window, with nodding approval, by PC254.

In between the dancing and singing, PC254 holds court as a tutor on the finest aspects of safety and law abiding behaviour. He livens up these discourses on zebra crossings by interjecting them with a succession of gags and rhymes. By the time of the second series there's a change of location. Now marching around the streets of a residential area, PC254 finds an old-fashioned bioscope through which he is able to watch the pop star puppets. And he's joined by young Adam, who lives in one of the houses along the beat. Taking Adam under his wing, PC254 tutors him in the ways of safety.

Denis Gifford wrote the first 13-episode series of *The Laughing Policeman* and, with a multitude of talents at his disposal, carved out quite the career. For one thing, he co-wrote Morecambe and Wise's first TV series *Running Wild* in 1954. But Gifford also managed to maintain a leading position as both a talented comic artist and an authority figure on the history of comics. Gifford was no stranger to children's TV either, having previously written for *The Witches Brew* and *Junior Showtime*. Gifford had departed *The Laughing Policeman* by the second series and was replaced by Gerry Andrews

Following on from Gifford's previous work in children's TV, it was Yorkshire Television who would produce his scripts of *The Laughing Policeman* for ITV. Taking up residence in the ITV lunchtime slot for children, *The Laughing Policeman* aired in and around other lunchtime shows such as *Pipkins* and *Rainbow*. The 15-minute episodes were, as with most of Yorkshire's output for children at the time, produced by Jess Yates. And the series was directed by Ian Bolt who would later direct episodes of *Under the Same Sun* and *The Book Tower*.

The colourful cast of puppets came courtesy of Roger Stevenson whose previous credits for Yorkshire TV included *Diane's Magic Theatre, Nuts and Bones* and *The Witches Brew*. Stevens discusses how he became to be with the series:

"My relationship with Yorkshire meant that we were constantly going

36

from one show to the next. And The Laughing Policeman followed on from Nuts and Bones. We had loads of puppet inserts recorded and we were looking for a vehicle to put these in. I think Jess Yates came up with the idea of The Laughing Policeman as he knew Deryck Guyler. I didn't get to meet Deryck on set as he had already recorded all his sections. But I did know him and he was a lovely man"

It only takes a cursory look at British entertainment in the mid-20th century to appreciate the contribution of Deryck Guyler. Appearing in BBC Radio's comedy programme *It's That Man Again* as Frisby Dyke in the 1940s, Guyler performed with what is believed to be the first Scouse accent ever heard on the radio. Guyler's most famous roles are firmly entrenched in TV comedy. His turns as the bumbling, yet lovable PC Corky Turnbull in *Sykes* and the pompous, cranky caretaker Norman Potter in *Please Sir!* both underline his legacy.

His ventures into children's TV were rather limited aside from occasional appearances on *The Sooty Show* and *The Basil Brush Show*. But *The Laughing Policeman* allowed him to perform directly to a young audience. And his character of PC254 isn't a million miles away from that of Corky in *Sykes*. However, whereas Corky was a disaster in uniform, PC254 is more assured. It doesn't draw upon Guyler's comic potential, but this time he's portraying an authority figure with plenty of messages on safety, so any pratfalls would undermine these topics.

The second series introduces Adam as PC254's young charge and gives Guyler's avuncular charm the chance to really shine. With a propensity for winning smiles and a natural delight in cracking gentle gags, it's a shame that Guyler wasn't more involved in children's TV. The main thrust of the programme is to impart friendly advice to the young viewers on the subject of safety. Thanks to Guyler's natural charm this is delivered with an authority which never feels overbearing. It's the epitome of those, seemingly now extinct, friendly local bobbies.

You have to remember, though, that children aren't in the market for a nonstop safety lesson. They need their learning broken up. And the best way to break it up is with fun. Enter Roger Stevenson's puppets. Crafted with intricate care and detail, this melange of marionettes are an eye catching spectacle. And, as with his previous work with Yorkshire, Stevenson's talent on the strings ensures a lively set of performances.

The world of constabulary advice and contemporary pop songs make for unusual bedfellows, yet there's an affable vein of entertainment within *The Laughing Policeman*. And where else could you find a green cat in an electric blue suit singing Daughters of Darkness? Nowhere. A true oddity.

JUMBO SPENCER

BBC1
1976

There's no finer sound, for a child, than that final school bell before the summer holidays start. The ringing signals not only a prolonged break from reading, writing and arithmetic, but also a world of potential adventure. And there's always some mad scheme to contemplate for the holiday.

Perhaps it's time to start publishing that homemade comic you're convinced will rival the Beano. Maybe it's an ideal opportunity to launch a car washing business and make your fortune. Most of these schemes, as you're aware, fizzle out after a few days in a haze of building dens, water fights and, later on, cheap cider. Occasionally, though, a summer enterprise comes up trumps. Especially if your name is *Jumbo Spencer*.

The summer holidays are here and, for six glorious weeks, Jumbo Spencer (Mark Weavers) will be free from the confines of Shoredale Primary School. However, Jumbo Spencer is not an individual for who rest and relaxation is a priority. He needs a project to keep himself occupied. And, usually, he has several ideas lined up, but this year he's struggling.

By chance his inspiration comes while listening to the radio. Jumbo listens to a story about a great reformer who put things right for millions of people. With the internal cogs of his brain pushed into overdrive, Jumbo immediately formulates his summer plan. He is going to reform the village of Shoredale; sweeping out vice and poverty while righting wrongs. And he's going to achieve this with the help of his friends Mike (Huw

Higginson), Maggots (Natalie Boyce) and Freckles (John Weavers).

But how will Jumbo go about reforming Shoredale? Well, Miss Mogg (Betty Woolfe) could do with a zebra crossing setting up outside her house, so it's time for The Jumbo Spencer Reform Club to grab their paintbrushes. And what about putting Shoredale on the map historic tours around the village for 10p a pop? Yet, for Shoredale to be truly reformed, Jumbo decides it needs a village hall. And, if he can raise a hundred pounds towards it, local philanthropist Mr Bennett (Geoffrey Russell) will contribute the rest.

Starting in 1963, Helen Cresswell penned a sequence of novels with Jumbo Spencer at their forefront. And, just over a decade later, television decided to bring the very first of these novels to life. Filming for the series took place in Luccombe, Somerset with Jeremy Swan on board as director. Swan had previously directed episodes of *Jackanory* and would later work on programmes including *Rentaghost, Grandad* and *Galloping Galaxies.*

Helen Cresswell needs little introduction in terms of entertaining children. And it's a trick she managed to pull off in both literature and television. Most impressive was the the sheer range of genres she tackled. *The Bagthorpe Saga* had its feet firmly entrenched in comedy. *Moondial* ran headlong into supernatural horror. And, finally, her adaptation of *Five Children and It* explored fantasy narratives in a period landscape.

It's easy to gush about Cresswell's legacy, yet not everything she wrote burned with a decades enduring intensity. And falling into this camp is *Jumbo Spencer.* The lack of recognition granted to *Jumbo Spencer* is far from an excuse to tar and feather its legacy. Instead, the series has a youthful charm which helps reignite fading memories of long lost summers.

Helen Cresswell was always keen to inject comedy into her work and *Jumbo Spencer* is no different. It may be a gentle brand of comedy, mostly concerned with Jumbo's gang infuriating the locals, but it helps to solidify the youthful exuberance on offer. Jumbo Spencer, himself, is a fantastic creation by Cresswell. With a maturity, eloquence and bow-tie far beyond his years, Jumbo marks himself out as a leader of men. He coolly takes control of the apparent malaise afflicting Shoredale and executes his plans like a seasoned project manager.

And the performance by Mark Weavers is a remarkable one. Weavers did not pursue a career in television and this must be considered a major loss for the medium. Whilst Jumbo is a well-rounded and engaging character, his peers fare less well and there's little to differentiate them from being friendly stooges. Although they're not the strongest supporting characters, they remain likeable. It's a sweet, idyllic world where there's very little to fear in terms of consequences.

Cresswell may have created stronger pieces of work, but *Jumbo Spencer* is unique in that it genuinely feels like time travel. The series takes you back to a simpler, carefree existence where your main concern was getting home in time for a barbeque. Nostalgia, of course, can be a rose tinting indulgence, but when it mines memories that are there to be cherished, well, it's a worthy indulgence. *Jumbo Spencer* is the perfect conduit to these memories and will leave you with a childish smile on your face.

KATHY'S QUIZ

ITV
1976 – 1978

The intricate and rhythmic melodies of music provide a constant soundtrack to our lives. There are the early lullabies our mothers sing us, the songs that shape our doomed teenage romances and, finally, the songs we choose for our funerals. This book, thankfully, isn't here to concentrate on the tragedy of our eventual passing. Instead, we'll use this juncture to segue neatly back into the thrust of children's television. After all, music has long been an essential staple of this arena thanks to its ability to entertain and educate.

And *Kathy's Quiz* sets out to achieve this with six strings and a trio of Northern accents. Kathy Jones, Noel Cameron and Lynn Garner are the purveyors of melody in *Kathy's Quiz*. Sat in front of a series of backgrounds – including snowscapes, gardens and grand lawns covered in fried eggs – the trio are here to play a game.

With an absence of complication, the game involves one of the presenters delivering a clue that relates to a mystery three-letter word. This clue can take the form of, for example, something you can find in food. The presenters lend a helping hand by using songs to identify the three letters that make up the word. The presenters take it in turns to sing one of the songs before revealing the letter in question and elaborating on its phonetic sound. Finally, just for fun, the presenters close the episode with a song or two such as There Was a Mouse and Pretty Little Black Eyed Susie.

Three series of *Kathy's Quiz* were produced by Granada between 1976 and 1977 with a total of 32 episodes, each running to 10 minutes. The episodes were broadcast nationally in the lunchtime children's slot on ITV. Only one repeat run was forthcoming and this was purely limited to the Granada region in 1978. Muriel Young, a Granada stalwart who also produced *Clapperboard, Lift Off with Ayesha* and *Shang-a-Lang*, acted as producer for *Kathy's Quiz*.

As Kathy Jones recalls, the series came about thanks to a previous working relationship she had developed with Young:

"I'd known Mu since 1972 when I was 18 years old. She had seen me around Granada working on a few programs since 1967. So, in 1972, she offered me a couple of pilot children's programs, one of which Granada took on called A Handful of Songs. I'd recorded a few series of these when I was offered the part of Tricia Hopkins in Coronation Street. I asked Mu if she would release me from Handful for a short while and, on the premise that I would return to Children's programs with her, she agreed. I ended up being in the Street longer than expected, so Handful was handed over to Maria Morgan in my absence and another program was drawn up, Kathy's Quiz"

Recorded at the Granada Studios on Quay Street, Manchester, *Kathy's Quiz* proved to be a straightforward production with few obstacles as far as Jones was concerned:

"The first time I met Lynn and Noel, we spent our time reading through the scripts and sang a few nursery rhymes. After selecting which keys Noel would play them in, we recorded them the next day in studio 6. Poor Noel always had to play my songs in much lower keys than expected

as my voice is quite low as I'm a mezzo contralto. From then on we would just turn up for rehearsals one morning and then, depending on studio time, record in the same afternoon or the next day. Usually it took about two takes, a tech problem, or a missed line from one of us, but sometimes on one take. We all got on very well which made recording much easier"

Certainly, *Kathy's Quiz* is located in an entirely different postcode to anything that approaches complexity. But that's exactly what the series is aiming for. Three year olds don't want to sit and discuss the linguistic mechanics of word construction in too much detail. Especially at lunchtime. Rather, they would prefer to have a quick dose of fun alongside a ham sandwich and, this being the 1970s, a drink packed full of E-numbers.

And, to help these young children achieve their objective, *Kathy's Quiz* has much to offer. The presenters are jammed full of talent and it's their musical skill that helps *Kathy's Quiz* escape its budgetary restrictions. Kathy Jones' operatic tones bring a bewitching set of melodies to the songs. Lynn Gardner's poppy vocals stealthily tap into your auditory system. And Noel Cameron's Yorkshire lilt and guitar work provides an agreeable bedrock for the songs.

Not all of the songs featured are instantly recognisable to British ears, so amongst the classics such as Hey Diddle Diddle you also get Big Rock Candy Mountain and Go Tell Aunt Rhody. Sitting nicely alongside the British pieces, they generate some variety in the musical compositions and language. At the same time, the guessing game (it's not really a quiz, is it?) is rudimentary fare, yet it's essential in providing a framework for the songs. It also helps to lay down early stepping stones in understanding the wonder of language.

44

A little more variety to the format wouldn't have gone amiss, but *Kathy's Quiz* avoids falling into a formulaic abyss thanks to the episodes' short, sharp running time. It may not be considered a stone cold classic of British children's TV, although, by virtue of the talent on offer, *Kathy's Quiz* deserves more than a mere mention in the history books.

HOW DO YOU DO!

BBC1
1977

There comes a period in every pre-schooler's life when it appears that the most honourable and pleasurable pursuits are counting, rhyming, listening to stories and kicking the family cat. It's an intriguing stretch of childhood. And one that, cat kicking aside, helps to develop a number of essential life skills.

Television executives are keen to use these building blocks of numbers, rhymes and narratives to engage young audiences and this explains why they're so prevalent in children's TV. If you add in some percussive magic and a highly engaging presenter then you get something very special. You get *How Do You Do!*

Fronted by Carmen Munro against a sparse backdrop illuminated by hues of yellow and orange, *How Do You Do!* is a combination of rhymes, counting games and illustrated stories. Munro isn't alone on the set of *How Do You Do!* She's joined by musician Greg Knowles on percussion duties. In what is a mildly surreal move, each episode finds a number of curious objects hanging down from the ceiling; it's not unusual to find Munro presenting in amongst dangling boxes of cornflakes and packets of soup. And these are used as focal point to shift episodes towards a world of rhyming magic.

A collection of hanging stars allows Munro to break into a rendition of Twinkle, Twinkle. And dangling elephants are the perfect excuse to sing about elephants standing on a piece of string. Munro also uses these objects to facilitate the counting games so, for example, she may challenge viewers to count the number of stars hanging down from the heavens. Knowles, too, is brought to the fore during these counting games with Munro asking viewers to the count the notes he bangs out on his vibraphone.

Amidst all this are the illustrated adventures taking place at Miss King's nursery school. Helmed by Miss King, the school is populated by ten children all with their own idiosyncrasies: Scott, George, Cheng, Sandra, Caroline, Kevin, Tony, Mary and the twins Annie and Louise. The narratives awaiting the children are gentle affairs. Annie and Louise dress up in hospital gear to treat a poorly Scott. A trip to the library goes awry when Mary loses her beloved doll. And a morning of rain leads to the children investigating a sequence of wet footprints.

The percussive, rhyming curiosity that was *How Do You Do!* consisted of 13 episodes over the course of a single series. The 15-minute episodes were part of the Watch with Mother schedule and repeats of *How Do You Do!* continued up until 1981. These episodes were written, produced and directed by Carole Ward, who had previously written for *Play School* and *Play Away* as well as presenting the former.

Greg Knowles, who had been recommended to Ward by the musician Elgar Howarth, didn't necessarily find working on *How Do You Do!* the easiest assignment to fit into his busy schedule as he recalls:

"I was a young kid from Preston, busy going all over the world with a lot of difficult and exciting music, so doing a regular engagement on TV seemed a hassle. Carole was great, obsessed with the kids counting games and all the graphics. When Carole was explaining the various shows she

was doing it with her hands like a puppet show. I couldn't see what was so important and Carole used to get really fed up because I hadn't read the script. I was so lucky to have been with such nice people and not to have got sacked"

Knowles recalls some frustration with the instruments he was provided with, but there was still room for some creative satisfaction as he explains:

"They used a percussion hire firm called Maurice Placquet because he supplied all of BBC TV. I used to give him a terrible time because I was never happy with the instruments. I was very young and a real prima donna. The music was just little jingles played on vibraphone or drums. I made it up at home and then we recorded it on set. I don't remember doing many takes. I wanted to write the theme tune but they got Johnny Pearson to do it. I did play the drums on it, though, which was done at Lime Grove studios. I enjoyed that because I had heard of Johnny Pearson, so I felt like a proper session player"

Kicking off episodes with the rhyming, clapping brilliance of the 'One, Two, How Do You Do!' song, the series instantly establishes its rhythm and approach through good old fashioned simplicity. And, with its formulaic structure, *How Do You Do!* certainly clutches simplicity close to its chest.

Carmen Munro is very much the focal point of *How Do You Do!* and her vast experience, having been a mainstay on British stage and screen since the early 1960s, ensures the show is in safe hands. Munro had previously presented episodes of *Play School* and *Play Away*, so she evidently understands of the importance of a wholesome, kindly disposition. Knowles –

whose speaking role is limited to merely saying "Hello!" and "Goodbye!" – doesn't exactly have his musical boundaries pushed during *How Do You Do!* But his abilities are unmistakable, with his vibraphone compositions specifically standing out as dreamy gems.

In terms of the content that the presenters are working with, it's far from revolutionary entertainment. But there's a minimalist beauty at play. Nursery rhymes such as The Owl and the Pussycat and Little Jack Horner have delighted children for generations and, no doubt, will continue to resonate for many years yet. And, coupled with Munro's effortless charm, it's rather redundant to ask for anything else. Likewise, the counting games, backed up by Knowles' percussion, are perfectly pitched to garner audience participation.

The final section of *How Do You Do!* to look at are the stories concerning Miss King's nursery school. Although they're unremarkable narratives, there's a pleasant charm that encapsulates those earliest learning experiences. And to a pre-schooler, these sections paint a reassuring picture of the academic world they will soon be entering. Meanwhile, Knowles' vibraphone theme which opens and closes the stories is a work of chiming brilliance.

How Do You Do! isn't one of those shows that has permeated deep into the memory banks. This isn't to say it's a series without merit. Carole Ward, Carmen Munro and Greg Knowles have all contributed towards an enjoyable programme. One that is more than capable, even if it's only fleetingly, of using time honoured methods to pique the interest of young viewers.

GRANNY'S KITCHEN

ITV
1977

Nothing tastes quite as good as home cooking. Except for food cooked in a Michelin starred restaurant. But who can afford that? Not this writer, that's for sure. And children, unless they're blessed with astronomical pocket money, certainly can't. But it doesn't matter. Home cooking is a great deal more fun.

And it's where we all learn about cooking, even if it is just the finer points of beans on toast. Taking a range of basic ingredients and turning them into something mouthwatering is tantamount to magic. That's why children are captivated by cooking. Yet turning a kitchen over to a child is far from recommended. They need supervision. And they need *Granny's Kitchen*.

Dorothy Sleightholme is the titular Granny of *Granny's Kitchen* and the landscape she inhabits is a traditional farmhouse kitchen. Packed full of all the necessary equipment required for the most basic forms of cooking, Sleightholme's kitchen appears conventional. However, look a little closer and you'll see that it differs from most.

Upon the Welsh dresser, for instance, there sits a music box. And it's a music box which is overflowing with nursery rhymes. Each episode of *Granny's Kitchen* starts with a nursery rhyme emerging from the box to set up that week's recipe e.g. The Queen of Hearts for jam tarts and There Was an Old Woman Who Lived in a Shoe for broth.

Following this rhyming fun, which is accompanied by

illustrations, it's time to look at another peculiarity of the kitchen. Just to the side of the Welsh dresser there is a tiny door. And it's decorated with a door knocker made from a spoon. Sleightholme knocks at it three times and, within seconds, a pair of children emerge. Donning aprons, the children are instructed to head to the kitchen table.

Here they get involved in making the recipe e.g. rolling and cutting pastry. Proceedings are soon brought to a close when the music box bursts back into life with a quick tune. But, before the children leave, Sleightholme rewards them with a basket full of that week's finished recipe.

Granny's Kitchen was a lunchtime children's ITV show which came and went with little fanfare. The thirteen episodes received just a single airing with no repeats built into future schedules. The series was a Yorkshire Television production with the 10-minute episodes opening ITV's lunchtime slot on Thursdays alongside shows such as *Rainbow, Pipkins* and *Stepping Stones.*

Mary Watts, who had produced *Farmhouse Kitchen* with her husband Graham, acted as producer for *Granny's Kitchen* whilst Joy Whitby presided over the programme as executive producer. Whitby, who had recently joined Yorkshire, remembers how the series got off the ground:

"My predecessor was Jess Yates who was focusing on Stars on Sunday and there had been family drama (as a freelance, I had script edited Boy Dominic). But I don't remember inheriting any programmes when I took over as Head of Children's Programmes in 1976. Paul Fox gave me a free hand devising new formats and Granny's Kitchen was one of the first productions. Dorothy Sleightholme had been fronting Farmhouse Kitchen,

a successful YTV cookery programme for adults, since 1971 and I thought it would be fun to produce a version for small children. One of my friends was Marion Lines, an inspired nursery school teacher and writer who acted as adviser"

Cookery programmes have been on the rise since the 1970s and this explosion in popularity seems unstoppable. Each time the format appears to have reached saturation point, a new angle is crafted in the genre be it sweary chefs or genteel baking in a tent. It's a television executive's dream, a simple format and one which remains low cost. Yet, the world of cookery has a limited presence in children's TV. Where most formats transfer seamlessly, cookery shows have struggled to gain a foothold. *Granny's Kitchen* is an early attempt to buck this trend.

Kitchens are dangerous places for young children, so our earliest experiences of cooking are simple affairs. There's no need to understand the finer points of filleting a monkfish and *Granny's Kitchen* acknowledges this with a range of simple recipes. It's a cookbook which has a strong emphasis on baking, although there's still room for egg salads and vegetable soups. The runtime is a little prohibitive towards any detailed learning, but the children aren't bothered. They get their hands messy. And that's a fantastic afternoon for any youngster.

Taking control of the kitchen is Dorothy Sleightholme and she's a formidable figure. Whilst she has the appearance and stature of a Yorkshire Granny, you wouldn't want to disrupt her kitchen. This strong spirit is crucial for manning and controlling a kitchen, but Sleightholme doesn't come across as a natural performer with children. Marion Lines, who features in the Sleightholme role in the pilot, feels more suited to the role. Nonetheless, Sleightholme still finds some time for joyful moments, such as dishing out baskets of treat, but they are in short supply.

Granny's Kitchen didn't define a new era for cookery shows, although it is a brave dipping of the toe into unexplored waters. The nursery rhyme angle provides an effective ice breaker to engage young viewers and there's plenty of messy, tasty fun to promote the idea of cooking. There was no second series for *Granny's Kitchen* and Joy Whitby feels that the show was better in terms of ideas rather than execution. But with 21st century shows such as *Big Cook, Little Cook* and *My World Kitchen* proving popular with toddlers, it appears that television is finally moving in the right direction.

CALENDAR KIDS

ITV
1977 – 1978

Regional variations to the television schedules are rare occurrences in the 21st century with most being reserved for local news and current affairs programmes. But, throughout the second half of the 20th century, their presence was more common. This was most keenly felt on ITV where the network was made up regional franchises.

One of the most famous regional shows to emerge in the 1970s was ATV's Saturday morning show *Tiswas*. It was, at first, limited to the ATV region, although its infamy eventually led to the other ITV regions picking it up. Some regions, though, were slower than others with this uptake. And, if you were watching in the Yorkshire region during the late 1970s, instead of Chris Tarrant and the Phantom Flan Flinger, you would have seen Mark Curry and Kathryn Apanowicz in *Calendar Kids*.

A mixture of pop stars, competitions, animations and making viewers' dreams come true, *Calendar Kids* is your standard Saturday morning children's TV show. Well, apart from its obsession with skateboarding, but we'll come to that a little later. The format of *Calendar Kids* contains little surprises with the main section of the show given over to studio sections featuring Mark Curry and Kathryn Apanowicz. Who are 16 and 17 years old respectively. Yes, that's right, 16 and 17 years old.

At an age where their peers are mostly communicating in unintelligible grunts, Curry and Apanowicz are presenting a television show. And they're remarkably strong. Apanowicz may occasionally stumble over her lines, but this is a small criticism against an upbeat performance. Curry, on the other hand, is next to flawless. It's unbelievable that he's only 16 years old. He not only looks like he's in his early twenties, but he presents with a confidence and affability most adult presenters struggle to achieve. Sure, he had been appearing on TV since 1969, most notably in *Junior Showtime*, but his precocious talent is astounding.

The main sections of *Calendar Kids* take place in a studio which is populated with two teams of children hailing from various areas across the Yorkshire region e.g. Beverley and Scarborough. These two teams compete in a succession of tasks that include making the most realistic stock car noise, blowing the best raspberry and using makeup to create the most authentic black eye.

In between these battling children there's plenty of room for special guests. Lenny Henry pays a visit to do his Muhammad Ali impressions. Alan Parker discusses his latest film Bugsy Malone. And Alvin Stardust reveals that he's trying to avoid the taxman. The features that venture outside the studio are a varied bunch, with an emphasis on making viewers dreams come true. This is why we find young Mark Ainsworth going toe to toe with wrestler Alan Dennison and Timothy Webster getting up close with a harrier jump jet for his birthday.

And, as it's 1977, the booming popularity of skateboards is promoted through several features over the course of the series. The history of skateboarding is put under the microscope. Budding skateboarders are shown the ins and outs of completing the most basic tricks. And, finally, there's a competition to win an actual skateboard. Yorkshire Television were unavailable for comment, but it's safe to assume that *Calendar Kids* was responsible for a catalogue of skateboarding injuries.

Skateboarding aside, there's very little rebellion within *Calendar Kids.* So, while it certainly went up against *Tiswas,* they were very different beasts. *Tiswas*, which eventually came to Yorkshire Television in November 1979, was anarchy personified and lasted for a couple of hours. *Calendar Kids,* meanwhile, was more family friendly with a considerably shorter running time of 45 minutes. Nonetheless, *Calendar Kids* contains enough variety and action to ensure that children in Yorkshire didn't miss out *too* much.

HEADS AND TAILS

BBC1
1977 – 1979

The gleeful excitement displayed in the eye of a child at the zoo is a marvel to behold. Children love animals, those alien-like creatures that live and act in such different ways to us. The inherent wonders of our animal friends are an endless delight, so trips to the zoo have always been a firm family favourite.

But getting to the zoo isn't always easy. And certainly not several times a year. So this is where television comes to the rescue. Nature documentaries, or David Attenborough as they are better known, have always been supreme masters in teaching us about animals from the comfort of our homes.

And, if you want to get younger viewers engaged, just add in a couple of songs and they'll soon be enthralled by these *Heads and Tails*. Narrated and soundtracked by the inimitable vocals of Derek Griffiths, *Heads and Tails* is an exploration of animal adaptations and behaviour. Travelling the length and breadth of the British Isles, with occasional sojourns to more exotic climates, the series looks at a diverse range of animals.

The animals profiled include cranes, highland cattle, red setters, flamingos and even humans. Griffiths is on hand to describe matters such as the interaction of red deer with local farmers, the locomotive action behind a sprinting dog and the age old magic of sheep herding. And there are songs. From the frenetic theme tune to folky pearls such as Gulls and Silence Too Has a Tale to Tell, *Heads and Tails* entertains throughout.

Heads and Tails came from the stable of BBC producer

Michael Cole, so, as you can imagine, its quality is almost guaranteed. The programme found its home, as with many of Cole's productions, in the Watch with Mother lunchtime slot on BBC1. *Heads and Tails* ran for two 13-episode series with repeats continuing on the See-Saw lunchtime schedule up until January 1988. The production was a popular one and BBC Records released a tie-in LP in 1980.

Heads and Tails also proved to be a favourite of Derek Griffiths and his memories of working on the programme remain strong:

"The series came about when I bumped into Michael Cole at Ealing Studios. He told me that he had a wealth of wildlife film he wanted to put into a series with my music, to his lyrics. I'd worked with him previously on Bod and Play School and he was so easy to work with. He was such a nice guy, so supportive and encouraging. Going back to Heads and Tails, Michael would send me the lyrics and film before I married them together in my music studio. We were asked to do a one man LP of all the music, I couldn't have backing girl vocals, so I did them myself. To this day people still think they were girls. Sad, eh?"

The formula behind *Heads and Tails* is simple: wildlife footage with narration and songs dubbed over the top. But you need a little more than simplicity for pre-schooler television to succeed. What you need is the magic of Michael Cole and Derek Griffiths. *Heads and Tails* probably would have worked with others on board, yet it's unlikely that it would have imprinted itself on so many memories.

And, yes, *Heads and Tails* is one of the more recognisable entries in this book. Nonetheless, it suffers from an unexplainable lack of recognition when it comes to looking at children's television. And this is baffling. For *Heads and Tails* is quite fantastic.

Wildlife footage may be ubiquitous, but this doesn't mean it can't be special. It is, after all, the most naturalistic performance that can be committed to celluloid. And it's an honesty which is simultaneously raw and beautiful. *Heads and Tails*, being a production for children, avoids the brutality of the animal kingdom and instead highlights its natural beauty.

The landscapes, alone, present an idyllic vision of the British Isles as coastal scenes rub shoulders with mountainous landscapes and woodland streams. But it's the animals that really shine. Honeybees clamber over flowers in full bloom while highland cattle roam the hills and bespectacled guillemots survey ocean seascapes.

The series is, coming from Michael Cole, geared towards education. But it's a brand of education which is infused with fun. Not that learning about animals could be anything less than a complete joy. So, we get to learn about the importance of a shaggy coat on Highland cattle and why a seal is clumsy on the land, but graceful in the water.

These are superb nuggets of learning, but then the songs take it to another level. And behind these marvellous ditties is Derek Griffiths. It's impossible to argue that Griffiths is anything less than a major figure in the history of British children's television. And, nearly 40 years after *Heads and Tails,* he can still be found on CBeebies in episodes of *Sarah and Duck.*

The music aspect of *Heads and Tails* is, not surprisingly, where Griffiths really comes into his own. His friendly tones chime perfectly against the menagerie of animal footage and, yes, those songs still stand up many years later. Whether it's a jazzy number about beetles scurrying across the desert sands or a song about an exuberant dog then Griffiths, with the help of Cole's lyrics, is on top form.

Heads and Tails is pre-schooler's television at its best. From the educational aspect through to the comedy voiceovers and melodic brilliance of Derek Griffiths, *Heads and Tails* strikes gold at every turn. Wildlife documentaries are now ten a penny what with whole channels dedicated to them, but *Heads and Tails* is unlike anything you'll see today. The programme is yet another feather in Michael Cole's cap and demonstrates how fantastic programmes can slide into obscurity.

MAGGIE

BBC2

1981 – 1982

Families provide lifelong relationships with an infinite number of ups and downs along the way. For every argument that has you threatening to leave there's a moment of tenderness which keeps you under the family wing. And this is why families stick together. Even if they are the most frustrating club you'll ever be a member of.

And, for a teenager, families can be especially testing. Balanced on the precipice of adulthood and independence, deciding your future is far from straightforward. Parents, of course, believe that they know what's best for you. But following the family blueprint is far from compulsory. Some teenagers want something different. Just ask *Maggie*.

Deep within the working class heart of Glasgow, Maggie McKinley (Kirsty Miller) is of school leaving age. In spite of this she wants to hang on for the Sixth Year. And, after this, she has her eyes set on university and a degree in social anthropology. It's an outlook which perplexes her working class mother (Mary Riggans) and father (Michael Sheard).

Maggie could, after all, go straight into a good job in an insurance office. And in a few years she could be married with a baby and a house, an aspiration which is very attractive to Maggie's sister Jean (Anne Berry). On a similar wavelength to Maggie is her brother Sandy (Paul Ferry). With ambitions of becoming a professional footballer, Sandy is determined to avoid following in his father's footsteps as a plumber.

Maggie's romantic life is also unrelenting in its complexity. In Glasgow, Maggie finds herself the subject of motorbike riding Mike's (Joe Mullaney) attentions. But Maggie is reticent to return his affections. And matters are made worse for Mike by the presence of James (Ian Michie). An affluent and intelligent young man, James lives in Edinburgh and is equally keen on Maggie's heart. Be that as it may, Maggie is unsure if she wants a relationship with anyone.

There's only one more complication awaiting Maggie: the family business. Following much prompting from Maggie, her father has set up a plumbing business with his pal Tam (Ron Paterson). The problem is that Maggie's father and Tam are far from businessman. And it's left to Maggie to handle the books and the admin. But will it be at the expense of her academic pursuits?

Maggie started life as a quartet of books written by Joan Lingard in the 1970s. The success of these books led to the BBC commissioning a series with Lingard adapting the first two books for the small screen. *Maggie* was produced by BBC Scotland and, unlike many Scottish productions of the era, went out across the UK in a primetime slot. Both series of *Maggie,* which ran to nine episodes each, were broadcast on BBC2.

The prestige of being broadcast south of Hadrian's Wall was, as Kirsty Miller recalls, something to celebrate:

"It did feel like a big deal. At that time the most depressing words heard on the TV were 'except for viewers in Scotland" So being on BBC2, in competition with Nationwide and on the front of the Radio Times, felt pretty special. It was also kind cool that Maggie was aimed at young

people, but went out in a later slot than Blue Peter and The Magic Roundabout"

Going back to the beginning of her journey as Maggie McKinley, Miller reveals that she almost passed up on the chance to audition:

"If I remember correctly, the BBC was keen to cast actors close to the age of the characters. They auditioned lots of young people from drama clubs and youth theatres like Glasgow Drama Workshop and Scottish Youth Theatre, both of which I was involved with. I believe I was the first person they saw and I very nearly didn't read. I was all set to go to university when they were due to start filming. To be honest, I was only planning on going to uni until I could get myself an Equity card. This was back in the day of no card, no work. Thankfully, after a few auditions with the other actors, I got the part!"

With such a young cast in place, all chomping at the bit of adolescence, youthful camaraderie was on tap as Miller remembers:

"We all got on great. I'm so pleased there was no internet and the tabloids weren't so focussed on TV stars because we got up to all the usual nonsense that young adults get up to. Anne Berry and I ended up sharing a flat, we moved in together between shooting series 1 and 2. Everyone was convinced we were going to rack and ruin. Which, to be fair we were, but hey we were 19 and having a great time!"

The world of *Maggie* should be familiar to anyone who has ever had to navigate the tricky seas of adolescence; that's all of us. The dilemmas facing Maggie may feel familiar, but this doesn't make them any less fascinating. Family, friendships and aspirations are strong themes. And *Maggie* weaves these into an absorbing look at teenage development.

At first it appears that Maggie is the epitome of confidence and self-assuredness. The opening titles, backed by B.A. Robertson's evocative theme tune, find her in fine fettle. Frolicking through the dilapidated streets of Glasgow, Maggie exudes a vim and vigour which promises great things. Joan Lingard's narratives, however, reveal that Maggie is stuck at life's crossroads.

And the scripts capture this unsettled state of mind with great precision and subtlety. It would be far too easy, and dull, for Maggie to slump into a clichéd teenage funk and then have her narrative rescued. Instead, Lingard crafts a story which allows the character of Maggie to grow organically. Sure, she makes mistakes by leading on both her family and potential suitors, but that's all part of growing up.

It's foolish for Maggie to head over to the local disco and dance with both Mike and James (to Ultravox), but who said romance was easy? And Maggie doesn't help matters at home by prioritising plumbing jobs over her schoolwork, but how can she let her family down? Thankfully, by the end of the second series, Maggie's experience begins to manifest itself in making more mature decisions.

And this growth is made all the more possible due to the excellent performance of Kirsty Miller. It's a portrayal which captures the whole, complicated spectrum of adolescence with nuance, charm and cheer. The cast list of *Maggie* is a little too large to mention all the performers, although there's enough room to give nods to Michael Sheard as the worrisome Mr McKinley and Jean Faulds as Maggie's wise grandmother.

The final point of interest attributed to the series is its setting. The threads and themes of *Maggie* may have been universal, but the sights and sounds presented by Glasgow, Edinburgh and Inverness-shire were entirely new to the rest of the country. Perhaps some viewers struggled with the accents, but, as Joan Lingard told the Radio Times in 1981, the Scottish had been dealing with Cockney accents on television for years.

And *Maggie* is a series that Scotland should be proud of. Marking a brave step into the mainstream schedules, *Maggie* is an authentic essay on the growing pains of adolescence. The landscape of *Maggie*, what with its lack of dating apps and social media, may appear outdated to the modern world, but the same core issues affect teenagers to this very day. A special watch.

ROWAN'S REPORT

ITV
1982 – 1983

Success for a schoolchild usually centres on good grades, winning the 100m at sports day and cutting a fine swap deal on football stickers. Whereas most children are content with these objectives, a small proportion of them aim a little higher.

Perhaps this is down to an innate talent. Or it could be powered by an unbreakable self-belief. Sometimes it's both. Either way, a precocious talent is one that should both be nurtured and recognised to encourage its growth. And, in the early 1980s, children's television was more than prepared to highlight these extraordinary young souls in *Rowan's Report*.

Headed by presenter Nick Rowan (real name Wingham Rowan), *Rowan's Report* is a documentary series that concentrates on a procession of exceptional children. Each child has managed to succeed in a particular field in a manner which belies their years. And Rowan is on hand to investigate the whys and hows behind this success.

Children featured include Leeds United apprentice Neil Aspin, a youth member of the CND in the form of Anna Malos, pop star Annabella Lwin who fronts Bow Wow Wow and a young stockbroker going by the name of Jacob Rees-Mogg. Travelling around the country, Rowan spends time watching each child in their respective environments. These surroundings are a varied selection and include fashion shoots, stock advisors offices and recording studios.

In 1982 the dole queue in Britain was building up to record

levels, but it was still possible to seek out fame and fortune. Especially if you had youth and determination on your side. But enough about Wham! What about those who were even younger than George Michael and Andrew Ridgeley?

Rowan's Report, which was produced by Yorkshire Television, investigated these phenomena across two series and 19 episodes. The 12-minute episodes were directed by Alistair Hallum, who also directed *Ad Lib, Heggerty Haggerty* and *Gammon and Spinach* for Yorkshire, with Joy Whitby in place as the highly experienced producer. Both series took up the 4.30pm slot as part of the Children's ITV schedule and received just a single airing.

Central to *Rowan's Report* was the man whose name graced the titles. Wingham Rowan had started his career in the media by writing a piece in The Sunday Mirror about the activities children could get up to in the school holidays. And this acted as a springboard for approaching television companies.

Following an early stint on late night Tyne Tees show *Check it Out*, Wingham found himself working at Yorkshire Television under the tutelage of Joy Whitby. After fulfilling his obligatory duties as a runner, it was time for Wingham to step in front of the cameras. His first role came as a roving reporter on magazine show *Ad Lib* which laid the foundations for *Rowan's Report*. Suddenly having a series built around him was, in Wingham's own words, amazing:

"This 12-minute gap in the schedules had come up and I don't even think I was consulted about it. Joy Whitby told everyone that she had someone who could fill it and that they could build a show around this guy. Anyway, I was called into the Leeds office and Joy said 'I have some good

news for you. You're going to get your own series. You start work immediately' I remember stumbling onto a train afterwards in a daze and thinking *'Oh my God! I've got my own TV series!'* These were the days when being on TV was an amazing thing. It was well before the internet and when there were only three channels. And, don't forget, I was only 21 at the time"

Wingham is keen to recall that *Rowan's Report* aired in a curious age for children's television. An era where inspiration was highly valued, but the age of the tie-in action figure was just around the corner:

"We used to turn with two transit vans and a nine person crew to do a shoot. You'd pull up outside some kid's council house and the spectacle of recording would stop the whole street. This was before the marketing side of things started to kick in. There was a real desire to educate, uplift and inform. It was the complete antithesis of 'How do we get a toy spinoff marketed to this segment of this audience?' Instead we were asking 'What can we do to inform and inspire?' And Rowan's Report was part of that. We were highlighting these kids who had interesting lives and demonstrating that the viewers at home could have an interesting life too"

Rowan's Report was conceived as a teenage take on *Whicker's World* and centres upon the social interest behind a succession of intriguing characters. And those featured in *Rowan's Report* are as intriguing as they come.

Jacob Rees-Mogg, in his first substantial television appearance, surveys the stock market (and antique silver) with the eye of a seasoned pro. Annabella Lwin talks with incredible intelligence about the furore caused by her infamous nude

68

appearance on a record cover. And, with an impressive nonchalance, water skier Andrew Rock discusses the regular occurrence of broken bones.

All of these would be remarkable achievements for any adult. But these are teenagers. Powered by a precocious drive and determination these are remarkable young people. Rowan, impressively young himself, is aware of their notable achievements and is intent on teasing out their idiosyncrasies. With a youthful and friendly brand of questioning at his disposal, Rowan manages to balance probing questions with an accessibility that older presenters may have struggled to deliver.

And, thanks to the category driven nature of the subjects, each episode is an absorbing case study of youthful talent. These are curious individuals – Jacob Rees-Mogg is one of the few 13 year olds to aspire to the position of Prime Minister – but their graft and determination mark them out from their peers. Instead of playing Space Invaders in a dinghy arcade, these children are modelling for Gloria Vanderbilt and working towards sporting pinnacles.

The success of the series' thrust hinges not just on Rowan and his exceptional young charges. Joy Whitby also plays a crucial role. Wingham Rowan remembers her as being a special figure:

"She was amazing, a real intellectual powerhouse. She absolutely embodied the idea of public service broadcasting. She believed her job was to entertain and inform. The Book Tower, for example, clearly encouraged kids to read. She was very good to me, very understanding and very encouraging. I always felt extraordinary grateful. It wouldn't have happened without her picking my letter out of a pile and sending a nice

reply saying 'Why don't you send me some of your ideas for shows?'

With each episode running to just 12 minutes *Rowan's Report* makes for a cheerfully brisk documentary series. However, it's also a mature watch. Never once condescending to the children featured or those watching at home, *Rowan's Report* is eager to deliver on its remit of inspiring and entertaining.

Sure, not everyone featured on *Rowan's Report* went on to fame and fortune – although many are still involved in their respective fields – but the message is clear that age is no barrier. And, nostalgically, it harks back to an era where teenagers needed much more than just a YouTube channel to be considered a success. A highbrow triumph.

WIL CWAC CWAC / WILL QUACK QUACK

S4C
1982

Childhood is the most formative phase we go through as we mould and adapt our behaviour to the world around us. In fact, there's so much going on that there barely seems enough time to pack it all in. Yet we somehow do. Humans certainly aren't alone in evolving through these early experiences. You only have to take a swift glance at the adventures of *Wil Cwac Cwac* to appreciate this.

Deep within the simple surroundings of a rural Welsh village, there lives a duck named Wil. Far from spending his days pecking at scraps of bread and floating on the village pond, Wil's life is more adventurous. Scraps of bread are out as Wil is served an almost constant supply of wasp porridge and spider cake. And pond-based flotation is replaced with April's Fool's jokes, a face to face confrontation with an angry bull and a nasty case of the hiccups.

Episodes start not within a nest, but within Wil's bedroom where, after rousing himself, Wil dons his trademark attire of blue trousers, white t-shirt and blue neckerchief. It's then time to head outside where a world of adventure is awaiting him. And, like all children, Wil has a loyal gang around him. There's Ifan the turkey, Huw the goose and Sioni the chicken. In true boyhood fashion, they're a foolhardy bunch who regularly frustrate and enrage the village residents.

The origins of *Wil Cwac Cwac* can be traced to a Welsh language book entitled Llyfr Mawr y Plant. The book was first published in the early 1930s and was jointly written by Jennie Thomas and J.O. Williams. It had proved to be a popular children's book, but how would it make the leap to television?

Robin Lyons, one of the founders of Siriol Animation and producer of *Wil Cwac Cwac,* takes up the story of how these traditional tales made it to the air:

"We set up Siriol Animation to make SuperTed. I was one of the directors of the company and wrote the scripts, directed the voices, handled the music and got involved with the post-production. Later I became the producer. S4C was a new channel with a strong political brief to protect and support the Welsh language and its culture. SuperTed was seen to be "Welsh" in a broad sense but it was created by someone whose first language was English.

For political reasons S4C wanted another series that reflected Welsh language culture and asked us to make a series of Wil Cwac Cwac based on characters from Llyfr Mawr Y Plant (The Big Book for Children). Although I am not a Welsh speaker I saw Wil Cwac Cwac as an opportunity. Wil Cwac Cwac was the first series of films I produced and I am very proud of it.

With guidance from S4C we put together a team. Urien William, a writer steeped in Welsh culture, wrote the scripts, Myfanwy Talog was our voice in both languages and Iolo Jones wrote some great music played on medieval instruments by Philip Pickett. The director, Beth McFall, was from London"

Wil Cwac Cwac was commissioned by the newly formed S4C – the Welsh arm of Channel 4 – and the five-minute episodes began airing on S4C in late 1982. Naturally, the Welsh language presented within *Wil Cwac Cwac* was impenetrable for anyone outside of Wales, so an English language was also produced. The English version, which again featured Myfanwy Talog on narration duties, eventually ended up being sold to TV-am where it would air in the mid 1980's. And, on TV-am's insistence of an anglicised title, it went out as *Will Quack Quack*.

Village life has, even in the most bustling village, a tendency to lean towards the unremarkable and the humdrum. And it's a landscape which strongly informs the universe of *Wil Cwac Cwac*. From the rustic charms of Wil's stone built farmhouse through to the 1930s garb worn by the characters and an absence of technology, *Wil Cwac Cwac* invests in a world which stays faithful to Llyfr Mawr y Plant.

All children, whether they're from a rural village or a sprawling metropolis, are contractually obliged to be mischievous. But there's also room for bravery and relationships. And Wil is used to reflect these youthful traits. One episode can find Wil demonstrating a lack of responsibility by gobbling down all of his mother's honey. But he's equally likely to be found protecting his friends from an angry bull.

The village setting, naturally, doesn't lend itself to the vigorous end of the narrative spectrum. Instead these are gentle, charming adventures that encapsulate childhood and the many lessons to be learned. And these episodes are propelled with a pleasing pace which, given the brief runtime, never feels rushed. Manning the narrative, of course, is Myfanwy Talog whose Welsh lilt infuses the characters of Wil Cwac Cwac with an exuberant, Welsh charm.

The English language version remains a fond memory for many people who were growing up in the mid-1980s, but Robin Lyons reveals that it had an appeal which spread far beyond the United Kingdom:

"Welsh speakers always said to me at the time that though they liked SuperTed they much preferred Wil Cwac Cwac because it resonated with them. It was a part of their childhood. It was not just Welsh audiences that reacted this way. SuperTed had better production values, marketing and licensing but Wil Cwac Cwac sold to more countries. Its stories about a group of children growing up in a simple country village and having to make their own fun was something that children in the Soviet Union, China and around the world wanted to see"

With a set of foundations built upon its Welsh identity, *Wil Cwac Cwac* manages to exude a universal appeal which is hard to resist. It's not the most famous television show to emerge from Wales, but *Wil Cwac Cwac* can hold its head high.

LET'S READ WITH BASIL BRUSH

ITV
1982 – 1984

If you want a child to develop then it's essential that you get them into reading. Firstly, it allows them to scour the television schedules for their favourite programmes. Secondly, it means that, many decades on, they can pick up a book on said programmes and relive their dusty memories.

This isn't a view shared by everyone. Parents and teachers feel as though reading should be applied to more virtuous pursuits such as classic literature. Nonetheless, television is far from an anti-educational tool. For many, many decades, educational programming has aired as part of the British TV schedules. One of these programmes aimed to enhance the nation's reading skills. Its name: *Let's Read with Basil Brush*.

From deep beneath the roots of a grand tree, within his subterranean den, Basil Brush is learning to read. Helping Basil to get to grips with the basics of reading is Mr Howard (Howard Williams). And Mr Howard comes loaded with a collection of stories featuring Pepper the puppy. The adventures awaiting Pepper involve hijinks aboard a pirate ship, hiding from his mother at the park and terrifying beachgoers with a crab. Although he's interminably interrupted by Basil's wisecracks, Mr Howard eventually finishes reading the story.

The end of Pepper's story doesn't mean it's time for *Let's Read with Basil Brush* to close the book on its learning. Rather, it's the perfect opportunity to consolidate the education with a child-friendly readalong version of Pepper's story. With illustrations from the story now featuring a simple text beneath, Mr Howard takes the lead by reading the text slowly and clearly. Each text is echoed by Basil in a rather more impish and excitable manner.

The final section finds Mr Howard putting up three cards, each containing a phrase from the day's story. Opening these cards up soon reveals a composite picture. But, owing to Basil's meddling, it's rarely a coherent composite. So, for example, you can expect to find a cat with the body of bumblebee.

By the time *Let's Read with Basil Brush* landed on ITV, produced by Granada Television for the ITV Schools strand, Basil Brush had been on British screens for 20 years. His first appearance had been in 1962 as part of ITV's *The Three Scampis*, but sadly not a second of this series remains in existence. Whereas all five series of *The Three Scampis* are missing from the archives, *Let's Read with Basil Brush* fares much better with all 28 of its 10-minute episodes remaining.

Barry Hill, who wrote extensively for *Coronation Street* from the early 1970s up until the late 1990s, created the scripts for *Let's Read with Basil Brush*. Additional material was generated by Howard Williams and also lending a line or two was the voice of Basil Brush, Ivan Owen. When it came to the Pepper stories – released as a series of books for teachers and parents to purchase – Barry Hill was joined in writing these by a selection of writers including Diane Wilmer, Sybil Marshall, Lesley Cryer and John Coop.

If there's an area of *Let's Read with Basil Brush* that teachers would struggle to define then it would be the chemistry between Mr Howard and Basil. You see, it's superb. And to break it down and analyse it in any depth would detract from its natural, buoyant brilliance. Howard Williams was no stranger to Basil Brush having first worked with him on *The Three Scampis* and, in the late 1970s, as his human 'assistant' in the long running *The Basil Brush Show*. A double act of the highest order, Mr Howard and Basil exude a comedic excellence throughout *Let's Read with Basil Brush*.

Nevertheless, this isn't an out and out comedy show. There's the small matter of reading. And, given the title of the series, reading should be the main focus. The Pepper stories, whilst only mildly diverting, deliver miniature narratives that five and six year olds should be able to get to grips with easily. And the illustrations, in particular, stand out with their bold, crisp aesthetics.

Despite being unashamedly joyous, the comedy and excitement distracts from the learning aspect of the programme. Basil Brush in full throttle is never going to be conducive to learning. And it was a view shared by contemporary teachers, their feedback indicating they were far from keen on the series as a classroom tool. Naturally, few children would complain at the prospect of fun and excitement at school. Therefore, it would be a highly popular teacher who announced it was time for *Let's Read with Basil Brush*.

While *Let's Read with Basil Brush* may not satisfy the majority of educational needs, it's unlikely it caused British school children any harm. Besides, comedy is an important skill for children to learn and appreciate. And if there is an underrated comic genius it's Basil Brush. He was coming towards the end of his original sojourn on British television, but *Let's Read with Basil Brush* does little to detract from his grandeur. So let's celebrate *Let's Read with Basil Brush* for what it is: a 10-minute rollercoaster of wisecracks and comedy.

EUREKA

BBC2
1982 – 1986

If it wasn't for the brilliance and genius of inventors then our lives would be in a sorry state. Almost every device or product we encounter is the result of someone inventing a solution to a problem. The need to spread knowledge amongst the masses, for example, resulted in Johannes Gutenberg's printing press. It was the efforts of that one man which allowed people, many years later, to read up on long forgotten children's TV shows. And, if you're reading digitally, you need to thank Jack Kilby for inventing the microchip. But who were these inventors? And what was it that led to their *Eureka* moments?

Initially presented by Jeremy Beadle - and later by Sarah Greene and Paul McDowell - *Eureka* takes a look back at the history of inventions. Coming under the spotlight are a whole series of inventions. There's the humble zip, the ballpoint pen and more complex designs such as pinball machines and film cameras. These explorations take place, for the first two series, from a standard studio setup. But, for the final two series, the action shifts first to the Eureka College of Higher Education and then to the Eureka Museum of Invention.

The presenters of *Eureka* aren't alone during this odyssey of innovation. Helping to bring the stories to life are a procession of 'players' who include: Madeline Smith, Bernard Holley, Sylvester McCoy, Mike Savage, Julia Binsted, Jacqueline Clarke and Simon Gipps-Kent.

These players come together to portray the various historical characters in a succession of sketches which combine facts with a dash of comedy. And this is how we come to meet Benjamin Franklin (Sylvester McCoy), W K Kellogg (Mike Savage) and László Bíró (Bernard Holley). One final member of the *Eureka* team is Wilf Lunn. Known as the Doctor of Alternative Invention, Lunn showcases his useless inventions such as a mechanical jaw exerciser and an automatic toilet roll dispenser.

The seeds of *Eureka* were sown in 1981 when Jeremy Beadle and producer Clive Doig collaborated on a BBC2 series called *The Deceivers*. The programme looked at the history of tricksters, cheats and swindlers. And the majority of the cast were made up of those who later appeared in *Eureka*. Only one series of *The Deceivers* was produced before, a year later, *Eureka* debuted on BBC2 in a 6.10pm slot on Thursdays. All four series of *Eureka* would air first on BBC2 before being repeated, several months later, in the late afternoon children's slot on BBC1.

We're so busy and caught up in our own lives that we take most things for granted. Take, for example, the zip. We use zips on a daily basis, but are we aware of how they ended up on the front of our trousers? The majority of us will answer with a resounding no. But a minority will cry out YES! And there's a good chance that this is courtesy of *Eureka's* enquiring scope.

It's a show that could so easily have stuck to exploring the usual suspects – and it does allocate time to moments such as Edison and the lightbulb – but it mostly looks to tell those little known stories. That's why we get to learn about the origins of Worcestershire sauce, chewing gum and deckchairs. It's an approach to programming which sparks a firm interest in children (and any watching adults) whilst nicely echoing the innovation of the featured inventors.

The stories behind these inventors benefit from the fantastic cast members who feature throughout the series. The stable of performers remain relatively consistent over the four series with only minimal changes. Not only does this endow the episodes with a pleasing familiarity, but it also takes advantage of the talent on tap. And it's a collection of talent which helps to elevate the show above its peers.

Sylvester McCoy, Mike Savage and Bernard Holley stand out in particular by summoning up performances that mix just the right balance of drama and comedy. And the rest of the ensemble regularly hit that sweet spot of engagement. It should also be noted that Simon Gipps-Kent, who departed this mortal plane far too early, burns brightly here and highlights just how much talent we missed out on.

The presenters mirror this quality. Jeremy Beadle exhibits his typical excitability and it's a genuine enthusiasm which colours the first series. Much like Beadle, Sarah Greene is only on board briefly yet, even at 23 years old, she demonstrates a natural warmth and cheer. Paul McDowell, most recognisable to the young viewers as one of the hosts of *Newsround*, is less excitable but interacts well with the players.

The man to thank for steering the good ship *Eureka* onwards through the choppy seas of the mid-1980s is Clive Doig. A man with a great understanding of how to make children's TV – he also created *Jigsaw* and *Beat the Teacher* – Doig's mission with *Eureka* is to make learning accessible. And he does this whilst writing, producing and directing it all. It's a tough ask for one man to take on, but Doig has a wealth of experience at his disposal and succeeds.

Combining intrigue, comedy and facts, *Eureka* makes for a

captivating half-hour which holds up all these years later. It also manages to pull off that rare trick of appealing to not just children, but also adults. The series achieves this courtesy of the rich curiosity running through its veins. A eureka moment of children's television.

CAPTAIN ZEP – SPACE DETECTIVE

BBC1
1983 – 1984

It's tempting, when daydreaming about life in the future, to picture a utopian ideal. One where the less desirable aspects of our behaviour have been extinguished by technology and advanced thinking. Unfortunately, the reality is that these traits are deeply ingrained in our DNA. And are likely to remain there for the entirety of human existence.

In spite of this, we shouldn't be *too* hard on ourselves. These negative attributes are just as likely to be found across the entire galaxy in every single alien race. And, just as on Earth, these traits often result in criminality. But the galaxy needn't worry. Wherever there is crime there is also justice. And this justice comes in the form of *Captain Zep – Space Detective*.

If you're a budding space detective then the chances are you dream about enrolling at the Space Office of Law Verification and Enquiry (SOLVE) academy. Those who are lucky enough to become a SOLVE student are treated to not only a fetching orange gown, but also enough Brylcreem to slick their hair back for all eternity. The SOLVE academy, though, is more than just stylistic choices. As Principal Jason Brown (Ben Ellison) reveals, the students will be shown a famous crime detection video from the SOLVE archive. This video will be a case study of a serious and complicated crime.

Brown is joined by scientific advisor Professor Spiro (Harriet Keevil) – replaced in the second series by Professor Vana (Tracey Childs). But the true hero of the piece is Captain

Zep (Paul Greenwood/Richard Morant), the ultimate sleuth of the cosmos. Each investigation commences with Captain Zep providing a brief introduction to the crime video and reminding the students to take notes. These videos find Zep, Brown and Vana/Spiro interacting, thanks to the magic of green screen technology, with a number of illustrated villains as they analyse vital clues.

Crimes under the spotlight include the murder of a silo guard on the planet Delos, the re-emergence of an ancient plague on the planet Santos and 117 mysterious deaths at Sirap's intergalactic space suit contest. Cutting back to the SOLVE students, Zep takes this opportunity to discuss the clues before solving the crime in a final video.

The intergalactic adventures of Captain Zep and his trusted crew first zoomed into our cosmos in January 1983 on BBC1. The six episodes of the first series took up residence in the 5.10pm slot on Wednesdays and provided 30 minutes worth of escapist entertainment. The second series of *Captain Zep* followed in March 1984 with episodes being transmitted on Friday afternoons.

Captain Zep was created by Dick Hills, who also took on the writing duties for the first series. And it proved to be somewhat of a departure from Hills' usual oeuvre. Hills had previously written almost exclusively for the world of comedy. And it was a career which could boast writing credits for Morecambe & Wise, Frankie Howerd and Tommy Cooper.

For the second series of *Captain Zep,* the scripts came from Colin Bennett who had concurrently been working on Central Television's futuristic children's show *Luna*. Less prolific with his scriptwriting than Hills, Bennett had more success in the world of acting and appeared as the caretaker in *Take Hart,* Andy in the aforementioned *Luna* and, many years later, in *EastEnders.*

Producing both series of *Captain Zep* was Christopher Pilkington who had previously directed *Take Hart* and would later produce *Hart Beat* and *Sebastian the Incredible Drawing Dog.* Paul Greenwood, who starred as the first incarnation of Captain Zep, remembers his days manning Zep One fondly:

"It was a long time ago, so I can't remember exactly how I got involved with the series. I was working at the BBC quite a lot back then. I'd recently been on the telly doing the sitcom Rosie, so I was quite well known round the BBC. I think I had to go and see Christopher Pilkington to discuss it, but I can't remember having to read for the role. Chris was terrific, really enthusiastic and, if I ever suggested something, he would always go with it.

Everyone involved was really lovely and we had a great time making it. I really loved the technical side of it, it was fascinating to me to be standing against a bluescreen and talking to nothing while pretending there was a river in front of me. I always remember the feeling of enjoying it so much. I really wanted to do the second series, but I had to choose between that and two years at the RSC. And, for an actor, working for that length of time was very attractive, so I went to the RSC"

The first thing to strike you about *Captain Zep* is the look of the series. Actually, scratch that. The most immediate aspect to leap out at you is the superb theme tune. Recorded by The Spacewalkers, and later released as a 7" single by the BBC, you couldn't ask for more in a musical opening. Packed full of synthesisers at their pulsating best, it's as if you're listening to the latest release by OMD before the middle eight arrives and the vocals shift into Syd Barrett circa 1967. Following on from this melodic brilliance, we're treated to yet more sensory magnificence in the form of the visual aesthetics.

For anyone who's ever watched early 1980s *Doctor Who*, the sets of the SOLVE academy and Zep One could easily have doubled up as acting grounds for Gallifrey's finest. In fact, Paul Greenwood recalls Peter Davison, in full Who outfit, visiting the Zep One set to shake hands with him as part of the BBC's publicity push.

As Greenwood referenced earlier, bluescreen technology features heavily and this leads us onto one of the most striking visual elements of *Captain Zep*: the illustrations. Designed by Trevor Goring, Peter Jones and Paul Birkbeck, these highly stylised illustrations are markedly different from anything else seen in children's television. With the artwork of 2000AD clearly an influence, the graphics are dripping with a nightmare inducing menace.

Talking of menace, the plots are overflowing with it. And murder. Lots of murder. Almost every episode finds at least one murder being investigated. And, in first series episode The Warlords of Armageddia, a grisly scene finds Zep inspecting a rock with pieces of bashed-in skull embedded in it. Adult stuff indeed, but the production is clever enough to keep the right side of gratuitous and there's very little that could be considered graphic. The maturity continues into the actual crimes which take in the complexities of political subterfuge, slavery and aggressive trade practices.

This may seem like a lot for children to take in, but the truth is that they thrive upon being shown this level of respect.

Children love to feel like adults. And it's important that television understands this. Sure, you can serve them a fluffy cartoon every now and then. But they also crave the opportunity to dip their toe into the adult world on occasion. If a writer and producer can respect this then they are almost guaranteed viewers which return each week. So, for everyone involved, it's smiles all round.

What's particularly pleasing about the execution of *Captain Zep's* premise is the interactive angle. Containing multiple layers of engagement, the series ensures that no one feels left out. The SOLVE students are fully immersed in the crime solving aspect. And the crimes themselves are tough nuts to crack. The viewers are also privy to a nice payoff in the form of a weekly competition where Captain Zep poses two questions about that week's episode. And, if answered correctly, the entrants will win a SOLVE badge. A prize which will make them the envy of their peers.

Guiding all this action amongst the stars is the crew of Zep One. Both incarnations of Captain Zep are officious characters, but Paul Greenwood and Richard Morant are talented enough to impart the character with a comedic lightness. So, while they may remain as cool as a cucumber under pressure, they are just as likely to be found struggling to open a voice activated door. And, ultimately, they're heroes in the guise of all the classic sci-fi swashbucklers. So, you know, you want to *be* Captain Zep.

Ben Ellison, meanwhile, keeps the comedic vein flowing as he munches into Astro Flakes for breakfast and references the 1970s hits of Joe Walsh as classical music. However, there's a determined bravery to his lighter moments. An aspect also shared by the scientific expertise of Professors Vana and Spiro who help to fill in the scientific blanks.

Future shows that tackled the interactive genre such as *Knightmare* would undoubtedly be more immersive, but *Captain Zep* does itself proud. The series brings a thrilling set of adventures which are blessed (depending on your love of the genre) with the iconic look of 1980s British sci-fi. And, in the tradition of all good television, it harnesses the viewer's full attention. A forgotten sci-fi gem.

DORIS

ITV
1983 to 1985

Cats live a luxurious and pampered existence that we humans can only dream of. Sure, the lack of opposable thumbs may mean they're unable to operate a remote control, but there's a lot to be said for an existence spent sleeping and eating.

It's reductive, though, to suggest that this is all that cats do. Naturally, a significant amount of time is spent taunting dogs at windows and digging up the neighbours' flower beds. However, as *Doris* is about to discover, certain cats are born into a life where reality is an incredibly malleable proposition.

Doris is a black and white cat who, like any other cat, is only able to communicate through a sequence of meows that mean very little to humans aside from "FEED ME!" Luckily, for Doris, the necessity of a human voice is inessential in the feline world. Coupled with her Converse wearing, ginger tom boyfriend Marlon, Doris is going to find herself getting into all manner of scrapes with nary a ball of twine in sight. Instead, Doris taking trips to the moon to tackle industrious mice, floating through the night sky in a giant spoon and trying to improve the romantic prospects of a lonely snowman.

Devised and directed by Hilary Hayton – the creator of *Crystal Tipps and Alistair* – 40 episodes of *Doris* aired over the course of two series in 1983 and 1985. Produced by Yorkshire Television (although the second series also credits Hayton Associates), episodes of *Doris* were five minutes long and aired daily as part of the Children's ITV schedule. The show was based on a series of books written by Hayton which had been published by Piccolo in 1982.

The first series of Doris featured animation by Peter Lang (who had created *Pigeon Street* with Alan Rogers), but Lang had departed by the second and was replaced by Martin Wansborough. Providing the soundtrack for *Doris* was the esteemed composer Derek Wadsworth whilst keyboardist Dave Lawson conjured up the electronic bleeps that act as Doris and her pals' meows.

Given the iconic status of *Crystal Tipps and Alistair* it's difficult not to compare the two series. And there are certainly a number of similarities. Both are dialogue free and the visual aesthetics share a common gene, but *Doris* doesn't quite have the iconic sheen of *Crystal Tipps*. The characters within *Doris* all feel, due to their simplicity, a generic and interchangeable. Likewise, while some of the backgrounds featured are highly detailed pieces, others are sparse affairs which feel rushed.

But you can't judge a book by its cover. And, in *Doris*, there's an intriguing set of narratives waiting to unfold. Whilst the lack of dialogue can leave you confused over the action, a pleasing dose of whimsy infuses the episodes. A case in point is the aforementioned 'giant flying spoon' episode. It finds Doris floating through a starry, dreamlike landscape on a pink, fluffy cloud before being scooped up by said spoon. These quirky, imaginative touches are present throughout the episodes – such as mice chiselling into the moon for cheese – and grant a nice departure from reality.

Combined with an ever-changing soundscape that can quickly switch from sublime, melodic hummery to synth based grandeur, *Doris* carves out a surreal and interesting spectacle.

And it condenses a huge amount of plot into just five minutes, kind of like a TARDIS narrative if you can imagine such a thing. This is why *Doris*, although not defining itself as a slab of legendary children's TV, deserves applause for its idiosyncrasies. A boundary stretching example of children's television and one which refuses to outstay its welcome.

MAGIC MICRO MISSION

ITV
1983

Computers, despite being ubiquitous in the 21st century, continue to excite and delight us. If we're not cementing and maintaining relationships through some form of computer then we're using one to order pizza or, more importantly, post funny cat videos to social media. Back in the early 1980s, however, cat memes were a long way off. Nonetheless, the dawn of home computing meant that there was an explosion of interest in computers as evidenced by television programmes such as *The Computer Programme* and *Micro Live*.

While these programmes had a vague family feel to them, they were generally geared towards adults. And, to the disappointment of children all over the country, there was little emphasis on the most exciting aspect of computers: gaming. In spite of this, tucked away in the schedules, there was a glimmer of hope for British children. Well, as long as they lived in a certain part of country. To find out more we're going to have to go on a *Magic Micro Mission*.

The crew of the Magic Micro Mission spaceship are on a quest to understand the world of computers. Adrian Hedley captains the spaceship and has a loyal crew at his command. There's the sardonic computer Prune (Hilary Minster), the 'squeezed into a tight silver cat suit' Jo Wheeler and, finally, computer expert Egghead (Dr John Barker). These adults are not alone in space. They're also joined by The Famous Five. But this isn't the Famous Five of Enid Blyton fame. This is

Mandy, Robin, Julia, Leslie and Stephen. And they've been granted the highly enviable task of providing game reviews each week.

The extent of *Magic Micro Mission's* outlook on the world of computing is far reaching and each episode brings a diverse range of topics and special guests.

The role of computers in music is a major theme and is revisited several times. Rick Wakeman turns up to showcase the magic of electronic keyboards. John Walters of Landscape gets Jo to, no word of a lie, blow gently on his electronic woodwind instrument. And Chris Sievy, the man behind Frank Sidebottom, demonstrates his 8-bit music videos. But it's not all music. A good deal of alternative content is available.

Computer games developers frequently stop by the studio, sorry spaceship, to discuss their latest wares. Most notably, the highly eccentric duo Groucho (dressed as Groucho Marx) and Piman (a bizarre pink creation with a lengthy proboscis) turn up to exhibit their family friendly, non-violent games. Jo gets to grips with domestic robots in the form of the HERO-1 robot, which is dismissed by Prune as a reject from a Tupperware party. And Egghead delights in his Jargon Gobbler section which strives to educate on the basics of programming.

The Famous Five review numerous games throughout the course of *Magic Micro Mission.* And they're showcased on an endless series of different machines, some of which are highly obscure – who on Earth remembers the Sharp MZ700? Being youngsters, the reviews aren't exactly insightful critiques on the finer points of gaming. Confusingly, their scores are often wildly out of sync with their reviews too. Nonetheless, it acts as a quickfire guide to the latest games. It also provides a fine excuse to watch guests such as Willie Rushton and David Gower playing Manic Miner and Test Match respectively.

Magic Micro Mission was produced by Central Television and ran for six 25-minute episodes. The series aired in a 5.15pm slot, but was only transmitted by a handful of regional ITV broadcasters. Only Central, TVS, Ulster and Channel Television carried *Magic Micro Mission* as part of their schedules. In other ITV regions the viewers were treated to shows such as *University Challenge, Calendar Fashion Show* and *Diff'rent Strokes*.

To those watching, certain features must have really felt like the future. Even looking back with hindsight, the series is generously filled to the brim with curiosity. Early glimpses of the internet are viewed through the power of the Viewdata system and the pupils of Light Hall School proudly show off the world's first electronic school magazine. And then there are the predictions. The rise of smart watches and smart cars are correctly predicted. However, the concept of a world where robots do all the factory work and humans stay at home doing 'brain work' is a little off the mark. For now.

It's clearly not all gaming, so *Magic Micro Mission* can't lay claim to being the first gaming programme. But it's almost certainly the first (and probably only) TV show to cover K-Tel's curious game Battle of the Toothpaste Tubes. So, for that alone, it deserves a worthy mention in the history of computer games on television. Educational and entertaining, *Magic Micro Mission* is a fine snapshot of where the nation's youth stood with computers in the early 80s. And it does it all without a single cat meme.

FAST FORWARD

BBC1/BBC2
1984 to 1987

The sketch show has, at least during the early part of the 21st century, all but disappeared from British television. And it's a modern tragedy that would have Shakespeare scrabbling for his quill. Shows such as *Not Only... But Also, Monty Python's Flying Circus, Not the Nine O'Clock News* and *The Fast Show* became much more than mere comedy shows. They were part of the national fabric and conversation. Sadly, this branch of comedy has been deemed too expensive in the modern age where budget is king.

The one last bastion of security for the sketch show is children's television where the format still manages to maintain a presence. And, if we rewind a bit, we can see how effective it is with *Fast Forward*. "Watch me, I'm a video!" proclaims the theme tune to *Fast Forward* and, although the format of the series has little relation to videos, there's plenty to watch. If the title of the programme suggests anything then it's that the content is going to be rapid. And *Fast Forward* has velocity on its side.

Sketches tumble from the heavens at an alarming rate. And they're in the capable hands of skilled performers. Despite a number of changes to the cast across the three series, the pool of performers remains relatively small. Those on board are: Nick Wilton, Floella Benjamin, Andrew Secombe, Joanna Monro, Robert Harley and Sarah Mortimer.

Starting with all the presenters in the studio cracking gags (or avoiding the terror of Tiny, the unseen dog), *Fast Forward* quickly moves onto the sketches. And they run the full gamut of comedy.

Quickfire sketches are prevalent, so expect to find a woman paying for one and a half bus tickets before the camera reveals the 'half' is for a disembodied set of legs next to her. Long form sketches are also welcome with ruler of the cosmos Thagar approaching nerdy Henry in the park to join him in his fight against evil. Meanwhile there's linguistic magic available which, for example, features a greetings card company who speak entirely in couplets. And, to add a further dimension of comedy, massed crowds of children are called upon to deliver their favourite gags to camera.

Fast Forward first aired on BBC2 in November 1984, but it wasn't part of the traditional children's schedule. However, seeing, as it aired at 5.35pm, it was close enough for children to follow on from episodes of *The Box of Delights* over on BBC1. This setup continued for the second series, but by the time of series three it had been integrated into the BBC1 schedule. Nick Wilton was ever-present throughout the entire run and explains how the series got up and running:

"I was in the revue group Writers Inc with the producer, Trevor McCallum. We met when we were both writing for shows like Three of a Kind and Not The Nine O'Clock News. A group of us decided to get together and do a show made up from stuff we hadn't managed to get on TV. We performed the show in rooms above pubs around London and in 1982 took it up to Edinburgh, where we won the Perrier Award. I was in the last series of Playaway (for 4 episodes) which Trevor script edited, and the producers decided to come up with a new format to replace it. Trevor

created Fast Forward and asked me to be in it. Floella Benjamin, the Playaway regular, was kept in the show so there was some continuity"

An adult may wince at the groaners on offer in *Fast Forward*, but to a child these are the building blocks of comedy. The series *could* feature complex political satire, but it would fail in the laugh stakes. However, show a woman in a restaurant being offered the chef's surprise, before the chef jumps out shouting surprise, and you demonstrate the mechanics of anticipation, misdirection and payoff. Aside from the groaners there are a wealth of comedy styles on offer. Linguistic exercises are mined for all their comedic worth, visual gags are plentiful and the Late Late Laser Linkup section allows stock footage to be reimagined with witty headlines.

And this fine material is elevated further by one important factor: the performers. Their performances are eye-catching and this isn't down to the tremendous colour schemes offered by their 1980s wardrobe. All of the cast exhibit a comic savvy which gifts the material a pleasing slickness. Nick Wilton stands out owing to the expressive range at his disposal. Andy Secombe distances himself from his father's comedic shadow with a polished performance – just take a look at his ventriloquist reading of the end credits. Floella Benjamin, too, is a marvel of engaging affability, but what else would you expect from one of the queens of children's TV?

Wilton is eager to recall that working on the series, and at Television Centre, was a blast:

"It was like a club really and I feel very privileged to have been a member. We had access to the BBC's huge wardrobe department so could

get wonderful costumes for the sketches. The Children's department was based in the East Tower and was run like a family. It was always lovely to pop in and see them all. We rehearsed in a big building in Acton, which we called the Acton Hilton, and there were floors and floors of massive rehearsal rooms. All the BBC shows rehearsed there - Drama, Light Entertainment and Children's TV so there was a real mix in the canteen at lunchtime. It was amazing who you'd bump into in the lift"

The disposable and ephemeral nature of sketch shows means that the majority of them tend to rapidly vacate the memory banks. This is certainly no indicator of quality. And *Fast Forward* is a fine example of just how wonderful a sketch show can be. It's all down to the sharp, innovative material available and a raft of performances which are finely attuned to the art of comedy. Sketch shows may be sorely missed in the world of adult television, but at least there are a plethora of treasures like *Fast Forward* for us to rediscover.

LETTY

ITV
1984

Determination is an essential trait for any child to get ahead in a world which appears to be built for the exclusive preserve of adults. But what happens when circumstances conspire to make life even more difficult for a child? Well, thanks to the adaptability and guile at their disposal, they become even more determined. So there's no reason why a child in a wheelchair shouldn't smash international smuggling rings and take on criminals with a penchant for Duran Duran records. While this may sound far-fetched, it's exactly what *Letty* does.

Letty Boot (Victoria O'Keefe) hasn't had the best of starts in life. Born without the use of her legs and restricted to a wheelchair, Letty has also had to contend with parents unable to cope with the demands of a disabled child. And that's why Letty has ended up living in the Meadowbank children's home. Run by James (Brian Croucher) and Margaret (Alison Forsyth), affectionately known as Uncle and Auntie respectively, Meadowbank provides security and warmth. Nonetheless, life in residential care can still be an uncertain existence.

However, with Letty's current crop of friends – Brian (Josh Elwell), Trevor (Marc Barfoot) and Cath (Deborah Smith) – life is about to become very interesting. After a series of thefts at Meadowbank, which include a goldfish, a Duran Duran record and some rollerskates, Letty and her gang decide to form a detective agency. Inspired by the adventures of TV detective Shoestring, Letty names the gang The Letty Bootlace Detective

Agency. Together, the team will combat not only the Meadowbank thief, but also a string of break-ins at showjumping schools and the smuggling of illegal immigrants.

Letty's activities don't go entirely unnoticed. And she soon rouses the attentions of not only Auntie and Uncle, but also Inspector Jones (Glynn Edwards). Although Inspector Jones soon becomes fond of Letty's industrious nature, he is equally exasperated by her ability to get involved with matters best left to the police.

Having previously written *God's Wonderful Railway* for the BBC1 in 1980, Avril Rowlands was no stranger to penning a children's television series. And, in 1984, she was behind the six episodes of *Letty* that aired on Children's ITV. Produced by TVS, with Anna Home acting as executive producer, the six 25-minute episodes of *Letty* aired on Wednesday afternoons at 4.20pm. Casting her mind back, Rowlands reveals the inspiration for Letty Boot and how the series got off the ground:

"I based the character of Letty on a close friend of mine who is disabled. Although the physical problems she's lived with have naturally shaped her character to some extent, she cannot be solely defined by her disability. She is an inspirational person with a zest for life and a refusal to allow her disability to get in the way of what she wants to achieve. My character of Letty reflects, I hope, those characteristics, including her sense of humour and ability to laugh at herself. With this in mind, I wrote the script and approached Anna Home, who I not only knew personally, but who had also commissioned for the BBC, and was the executive producer on my children's drama series, God's Wonderful Railway"

Due to the TVS archive exchanging hands several times since their ITV franchise ended in 1992, it's not entirely clear whether the master tapes of *Letty* still survive. At some point, all the paperwork relating to the TVS back catalogue went missing and the majority of this material is mired in legal complications. As a result of the commercial shortcomings this has placed on the archive, certain shows have been wiped by the current archive holders. By chance, Avril Rowlands made home recordings of *Letty's* original broadcasts and these have been transferred for prosperity by the archivists Kaleidoscope.

Letty brings a refreshing narrative to the world of children's TV. The unique set of circumstances of disability and life in a children's home had, up until that point, rarely featured in the children's schedules. And the focal point of the series falls upon Letty and the trials and tribulations of being disabled.

Her frustrations are fully explored with not only the physical restrictions, but also the mental stresses of disability being placed under the spotlight. Brian, meanwhile, who is on the cusp of adoption, struggles to deal with a history of rejection in care. And young Jim has to battle homesickness as he adjusts to life in the care system.

Meadowbanks, of course, is central to all of these narratives. Avril Rowlands is keen to expand on the importance of the children's home in *Letty*:

"The idea of setting the story in a children's home arose because I needed Letty to be surrounded by other children. Because of her disability, meeting friends after school might have proved problematic. She would have been unlikely in those days to have been able to hang out on the streets with a group of friends and meeting at youth clubs etc. would have required

101

someone taking her and bringing her back. So a children's home was ideal. It also provided the necessary deeper background in respect of the attitude of her parents and the fact that while other children came and went, Letty remained behind"

With a universe established, it's time for Letty's crime fighting to begin. These investigations progress nicely in terms of criminal severity and each one has a couple of episodes dedicated to its cause, so there's room for the stories to breathe. The case of the missing goldfish acts as an introduction to what is very low level crime, yet it activates a desire for justice in Letty; it soon leads to more serious crimes being investigated. And, with these stakes raised, the danger that Letty places herself and her friends in begins to escalate.

These narratives are all performed with great talent by a cast which mixes youthful vigour with experienced skill. Glynn Edwards and Brian Croucher both deliver worthy performances steeped in charm. At the same time, Jamie Foreman and Billy Murray flex their trademark Cockney villain muscles as a pair of immigrant smugglers. Letty's fellow detectives in the crime agency may not have gone on to establish themselves as actors, but there's a pleasing chemistry between them which helps gee the narratives along and, together, they provide ample emotional introspection.

As regards Victoria O'Keefe's performance, this deserves a special mention. The initial plan had been to cast a disabled actor as Letty, but the rigours of insurance meant this was unviable. Instead, O'Keefe – who spent time preparing for the role with three young disabled men at Pinderfields Hospital – was selected to play Letty Boot. And it's a role that O'Keefe takes on with a determined and confident performance. Coupled with her emotive portrayal, in the same year, of Jane in nuclear drama *Threads*, it underlines the tragedy of her death in a traffic accident in 1990 at the age of 21.

Avril Rowlands has, in *Letty,* created a series all about marginalised characters. And this applies to both the real world and the world of television. Coupled to a pacy set of narratives, *Letty* redefines what a hero can be. Seamlessly mixing light and dark moments, *Letty* is a triumph of what children's television can be about.

TICKLE ON THE TUM

ITV
1984 – 1988

A trip down to the local post office, if you're lucky enough to still have one, is a quintessentially British experience. Not only are there interminable queues which remain courageously polite, but the local gossip on offer is scintillating. Just occasionally, though, you may be lucky enough to step into a very special post office. One where there are endless music, storytelling and laughter. And, if you want to experience such joviality, all you need to do is pull out a map and make your way to *Tickle on the Tum*.

Down in the town of Tickle, upon the river Tum, a world of stories, songs and jokes is unfolding. And it's all happening in the General Store and Post Office. Staffed at first by Ralph McTell and Danusia Harwood (later replaced by Jacqueline Reddin) the shop welcomes in the many and varied inhabitants of Tickle to tell their stories.

Dora (Penelope Keith) the bus driver regales viewers with a tale about her bus running out of fuel. Local pet shop owner Bunny Brown (Nerys Hughes) finds herself on the trail of a vegetable thief. And Dr Dimple (Bill Oddie) has to unravel the medical mystery of a young boy unable to laugh. Following the conclusion of each story, it's time for a quick round of jokes sent in from school children e.g. What do you a give a pig when it's ill? Oinkment! With these groaners out of the way, Ralph dusts down his guitar (or occasionally a banjo) to perform a song relating to that week's story.

Whilst this format mostly remains the same for the first three series, the final series sees a number of changes. Most notably, Ralph has departed. And the post office is now long gone. Jacqueline, however, remains centre stage. But her place of employment is now at the Tickle Broadcasting Corporation studios. Jacqueline isn't alone amongst the mixing desks and computers of TBC. She's joined by Dexter, the cat with something extra.

A total of four series of *Tickle on the Tum* were produced by Granada Television with over 100 10-minute episodes being transmitted. The show went out as part of the Children's ITV schedule with episodes airing in both the lunchtime and late afternoon slots. Patricia Pearson, who was one of several producers during the show's run, tells how she became involved with *Tickle on the Tum:*

"When Tickle on the Tum was first made, I had been a director of many different kinds of programmes for Granada. My main claim to fame was that I was the very first woman to direct the OB cameras at a broadcast football match in 1977. Because I was considered to be a competent live action director, I became involved with many of the varied studio productions from World in Action, election debates, quiz shows and children's programmes. Granada was a very inclusive company, I knew Stephen Leahy very well, and he just asked me if I would care to direct his new baby, Tickle on the Tum. It sounded great fun, and so I said yes please"

Rick Vanes wrote extensively for the second and third series of *Tickle on the Tum* and recalls how he came on board:

"I knew Pat Pearson and Steve Leahy, so they must have mentioned my name and experience to Martyn Day, who was producing the new series. He approached me and asked me to write the series, and since I was able to fit it in with my other work, I signed up. The Tickle stories were written by a variety of people - and what I was required to do was to build an episode around a story, structuring the episode so that it could also include a Ralph McTell song, and writing the dialogue for Ralph, Jacqueline Reddin and the special guest. It required craftsmanship more than out-and-out creativity. In the other shows, I had created the characters, given them their quirks and personalities, and developed them throughout the series (in partnership with the actors/puppeteers) so that they changed and grew"

The best place to start with *Tickle on the Tum* is with the driving force of the programme: the presenters. Highly skilled as a folk musician, Ralph McTell brings a wealth of laidback charm to the show. Whilst his acting certainly isn't the strongest on show, he weaves all the sections together with a deft and friendly hand.

Danusia Harwood, too, invests heavily in the engagement stakes to come up with a friendly brand of presenting. Yet it's with Jacqueline Reddin's upbeat charms that McTell strikes up a real chemistry. It would be an absolute pleasure to walk into any shop and find them behind the counter. But when you also have them perched on the stairs singing gentle songs it becomes very special.

This affable charm spreads throughout the entire format of *Tickle on the Tum*. Featuring the three key elements of entertaining young children – stories, songs and jokes – there's little time for errant attentions to go wandering. The shop setup also allows the series to have a revolving door policy. One which brings an endless stream of characters into the episodes.

And the cast are exceptional. It's an exhaustive list of performers that most primetime shows would kill for. Where else would you find Penelope Keith, Bill Oddie, Molly Sugden, Nerys Hughes, Billy Connolly and Tim Healy rubbing shoulders? The answer is simple: only in *Tickle on the Tum*. And it's not surprising to discover that this talent shines so brightly.

For Patricia Pearson, the cast were the perfect team to work with:

"I really have to say that none of the guest stars presented any problems whatsoever. They all entered completely into the spirit of the show, due in no small part to the gentle and warm character of Ralph McTell, and also the decidedly fun atmosphere that we created during the recordings"

Without Ralph McTell at the helm, though, how does the final series fare? Well, Jackie maintains the high standards she's set in the preceding series. And the wisecracking Dexter brings a new dynamic. The special guests, meanwhile, continue to rain from the heavens. Despite these plusses, *Tickle on the Tum* doesn't feel the same in its final incarnation. The introduction of technology in the form of the Tickle Broadcasting Corporation is a major sticking point. The previous three series had been infused with an olde worlde charm, but this new landscape lacks the same warmth and familiarity. And, of course, there's a big Ralph McTell shaped hole.

The series retains a cult audience and, even for those who failed to catch it at the time, it represents a superb helping of children's TV. With brevity on its side, *Tickle on the Tum* manages to condense a wealth of entertainment into its 10-minute runtime. And what more could you want?

THE LITTLE GREEN MAN

ITV
1985

The concept of alien life is a most intriguing one for small children. The ability to fly halfway across the galaxy in a spaceship covered in bright, flashing lights is clearly exciting. Factor in the unknown wonders of an alien and it's an attractive proposition for the imagination of any child. Unfortunately, meeting and making friends with an alien rarely becomes a reality for any child. Unless, of course, they're fortunate enough to receive a visit from *The Little Green Man*.

Sitting in a comfy armchair one evening, Sidney Keets (Skeets to his friends) is busy with an engrossing read. But, suddenly, his concentration is broken. There's an unusual commotion outside his window. Poking his head out the window, Skeets is in for a shock. The cause of all this noise is a hyper-illuminated spaceship. And it's landing in his garden. Despite the enormity of the situation, Skeets is far from petrified. Instead he rushes outside to discover who this intergalactic invader is. It's the Little Green Man.

Taking the exact shape and form of his moniker, the Little Green Man talks in an unintelligible jabber. Thankfully he seems friendly enough. Greenie, as Skeets calls him, is not alone. He's also joined by his companion Zoom Zoom, a little ball of yellow energy who levitates from place to place. Greenie has travelled from the planet Zombazan, described as a great way off, and is on an important mission. The curious inhabitants of Zombazan want to learn about the children of

Earth and their myriad peculiarities.

Together, Skeets, Greenie and Zoom Zoom will go on a string of adventures (narrated by Jon Pertwee) which take full advantage of Greenie's powers. Not only will they bring snowmen to life, but they will also go through the looking glass and take a trip to the circus.

A 13 episode solitary series, *The Little Green Man* was produced by Central Television for Children's ITV. Matthew Smith, better known as an authority figure on the JFK assassination, devised the programme and wrote the episodes. The 10-minute episodes, as with many of their ITV peers, were initially transmitted in the 12pm slot before being repeated later that day at 4pm.

The Little Green Man, as with many creative endeavours, was born from frustration. Bored with the grind of administrative duties as a lecturer, Smith found himself repeatedly doodling a strange little character on his pad. And, following repeated interest from the office staff, Greenie was born. Jon Pertwee came to the production having previously worked with Smith on an animated pilot titled The Adventures of Sir Ned the Knight.

More pleasingly, for Smith, *The Little Green Man* managed to pull in 7.5 million viewers at one point. And there was even a wealth of merchandise produced such as books, pyjamas and a hard boiled Greenie lolly. Despite this success, the machinations of television production and contracts meant that Smith had to stump up his own money to bankroll the show. This proved an unviable scenario for Smith's bank balance and there was no follow up series despite Central pushing for more.

The Little Green Man could, if it wanted, fly into space every week on an intergalactic adventure. But it chooses to, mostly, stay on Earth. After all, Greenie is there to learn about the planet. Thankfully this does little to restrict the boundaries of the narrative. And the show relishes the chance to dive headfirst into a world of whimsy and surrealism.

Children have always, even before Raymond Briggs came along, wanted their snowmen to come to life. And *The Little Green Man* is more than happy to indulge in this type of magic. Likewise, the episode that sees Greenie and Skeets go through the looking glass is clearly indebted to the surreal styles of Lewis Carroll. These unusual aspects all combine in a workout which flexes the imagination to its limits.

And, as with all good children's TV, there's a healthy dose of morality infused within the narrative pursuits. Skeets, Greenie and Zoom Zoom are falling over themselves to help people. They rescue families on the precipice of drowning, help a duke raise funds to maintain his castle and even lend a hand to save some children from a burning building. It's an exercise in altruism at its finest.

These adventures are driven by the participation of Jon Pertwee. For several generations of children he was a regular on television as either Doctor Who or Worzel Gummidge. And his talents are more than evident here. With a voice that is pitch perfect for bringing animations to life (see also *Superted*), Pertwee's eccentric, burbling lilt brings an immediate individuality to the characters.

Pertwee's vocal magnificence is complemented by Matthew Smith's melodic soundtrack. It may be simple, but the jaunty, jangling synth melodies sum up the gentle brilliance of the series. And the theme tune is fantastic. Kickstarted by a jaunty and infectious burst of whistling, it soon segues into a chorus of children (pupils from the Trinity Comprehensive School, Nottingham) singing over what sounds like an old time fairground organ tune. You'll be humming it for weeks after hearing it.

Sound wise, *The Little Green Man* is superb, but what about the animation? Well, it's a curious affair. The main characters are simplistic, yet they deliver a cute aesthetic. The backgrounds are a more mixed bag. Some are highly detailed with lovely watercolour flourishes, but others lack personality. However, It would be harsh to condemn the programme for a few indiscretions around the animation. Especially when it delivers in so many other areas.

So, quite rightly, we'll overlook this as there is a lot to celebrate about *The Little Green Man*. A quirky and winsome appeal is deeply ingrained in the series and it deserves more recognition. A marvellous addition to the chronicles of British children's TV.

THE GIDDY GAME SHOW

ITV
1985 – 1987

Childhood is full of challenges. And some are slightly more fun than others. Games, for example, are enormous fun. They also have the added bonus of helping to develop all manner of skills be they physical, moral or psychological. The combination of entertainment and development is a classic proposition for children's TV, so game shows have become a staple of the form. But how often do you find one that contains an observatory, a professor, a gorilla and an alien? The truth is it's not that often. Unless you're watching *The Giddy Game Show*.

Underneath a starlit sky, an observatory sits upon a hillside. But rather than admiring far and distant galaxies the inhabitants are indulging in a series of games. The white haired and bespectacled professor Gus (Richard Vernon) is joined in presenting these games with his colleagues Gorilla (Bernard Bresslaw) and the little green alien Giddy (Redvers Kyle) who zips around on a magic wand. And with cries from our triumvirate of "Gorilla's ready!", "Giddy's ready!" and "Gus is ready!" it's time for the games to begin.

Each episode is split into several different games which test the skills of the viewers. The matching game, for example, asks the viewer to match an object to a particular character from the theatre e.g. a lamp to Aladdin. Visual awareness skills are put to the test via a route finding game. This asks the viewer to navigate the correct route through a scene such as the safest path through a mass of battling cowboys and Indians.

Meanwhile, phonetic skills are taken care of by the alphabet game. Viewers are tasked with matching pictures that all start with the same letter to a unique description e.g. "Which picture is something you hit a ball with? Racket!"

A final game comes in the form of a weekly serial under the title of The Thrilling Adventures of Princess Galaxzena. Much like Giddy, Princess Galaxzena is a green alien who can fly, but her method of propulsion appears to be entirely innate. Each "terrifying space odyssey" as the narrator describes it requires Galaxzena to complete a task in one of the many corners of the universe. This can range from stifling the dreaded yawns on the planet Snoronia or retrieving five lustrous ladybirds from the Laser-men of Luminatus.

The premise behind *The Giddy Game Show* is an intriguing one. But where did this curious idea come from? Well, The origins of *The Giddy Game Show* can be found within an idea first put forward by Peter Schreck, an inventor who had developed a banana-shaped wand that could interact with television programmes. Although the technology could not be put to use in *The Giddy Game Show* it was, as producer and writer Joy Whitby remembers, enough to generate a full series:

"When Peter Schreck was developing his interactive technology he approached me at Yorkshire Television. A game show seemed the best way of trying out his ideas and our sound engineers were intrigued. They agreed to pioneer the project but as the interactive difficulties and costs increased they withdrew their support. The programme was really ahead of its time. I think we transmitted it in a conventional way because I don't remember distributing any wands to our audience. Our aim was to provide an original kind of experience for young viewers in which they could take an

114

active part by solving puzzles and participating in question and answer games. The games were fun but also educational in that they promoted cognitive skills like learning the letters of the alphabet, recognising shapes and making visual connections"

Whitby was joined on writing duties by two script consultants, Donald Davis and Marion Lines. Both, as Whitby is keen to stress, were integral to the finished product:

"Donald Davis was an artist friend who was also an amateur mimic with a great sense of humour. Marion Lines was a teacher of young children at Fox School and I had worked with her before - she was a published poet and also a hands-on artist who wrote and produced their school plays. They both contributed ideas and did voice-overs for the programmes. We met to devise the format together and they continued to help with the scripts"

The Giddy Game Show first made its presence known with the commencement of its opening series on 19th September 1985. The ten-minute episodes, which went on to make up three individual series, aired first at lunchtime and then in the late afternoon Children's ITV schedule. Television wasn't the only medium touched by *The Giddy Game Show*. There was also a computer game. Produced by Mirrorsoft in 1985, the cassette-based game featured four games based around learning. Computer magazine Electron User was a fan and stated that it provided "A lot of good bytes for your money" in its review.

For those who were there, avidly watching as they slurped from a glass of Ribena, *The Giddy Game Show* holds fond memories. The mere mention of the show's title is enough to elicit cries of "Gorilla's ready!" and "Game over!" from those of a certain age. It's not hard to see why pre-schoolers of the mid-1980s would take it to their hearts in such fashion. Sure, the underlying objective is one of learning, but it's wrapped up in an easily digestible layer of fun.

The matching games, for example, are simple affairs, but they're characterised by Gorilla's comedic interruptions. And the games are despatched with a pace which ensures their simplicity never becomes tedious. Nonetheless, it's unlikely that older viewers would have been even remotely tested by the games in offer. Quite why *The Giddy Game* show made the leap to the afternoon slot is a little puzzling. But it's plausible they would have welcomed a quick dose of easy thinking following a hard day at school. Regardless, it's a show for pre-schoolers and perfectly pitched for their developing cognitive skills.

There's no doubt that all of the games featured could have been (and almost certainly were) played between the viewers and parents in some form, but television has never been about replacing parental figures. While interactive learning is crucial between parent and child, it's also important for children to understand that learning can take many forms. And, yes, this can include watching Princess Galaxzena fly around the galaxy in search of scarab beetles.

Other game shows from the history of children's television may be better remembered (and contain more gunge tanks) but these tend to be the ones that focus on pure entertainment. *The Giddy Game Show* is a very different beast. Joy Whitby was always a proponent of using television to educate and *The Giddy Game Show* is typical of this outlook. It may not have fulfilled its original potential for interactive TV, yet it retains a nostalgic glee for many of the viewers who tuned in. And there's no finer benchmark of a series' success than that.

STILGOE'S ON

BBC1
1986

Back in the mid-1980s, the concept of being a child and being stuck inside was nothing short of a disaster. There was no YouTube, no Netflix and children's television, although fantastic, was limited to just a few hours a day. If you were lucky, you may have had a ZX Spectrum or a VHS player to pass the time, but even then you were limited to a certain number of tapes. So, if you were trapped inside due to torrential rain or even a day off school with the sniffles, you had to get a little inventive to stop going out of your mind.

Luckily, coming to your rescue was Richard Stilgoe with proof that, even in the most trying circumstances, life *Stilgoe's On.* Armed with just pens, crayons, scissors, a small forest's worth of paper and a Yamaha DX7, Richard Stilgoe is on a mission to stop you feeling woe begone when you're stuck indoors. And he's going to achieve this with a collection of tips, wordplay, games and magic. Each episode has a rough theme to structure its various activities around. So, you can expect to find episodes built around magic, how to have a party and that curious favourite of spots and dots.

The pursuits on offer are a varied bunch. Enthusiastic and industrious children get to grips with constructing robots out of old cereal boxes and tinfoil. The creation of a code wheel allows the kids to formulate and decipher fiendish codes. And there's also time to make a big bowl of coconut ice. Joining Stilgoe in the studio each week is a special guest. You can expect to find Paul Jackson the 'origami man' turning up to show children how to make a paper hat. Ray Alan serves up the laughs with Lord Charles. And who wouldn't want to meet the marionette magic of The Puppeteers' Company?

When it comes to Richard Stilgoe and children's TV, most people immediately think of *Finders Keepers.* It ran for five series throughout the early to mid-1980s and established Stilgoe as a curator of fun. But *Stilgoe's On,* coming a year later, struggles to gain the same recognition. It only ran for a single series of eight episodes on BBC1, so this lack of recall isn't a huge surprise. But it did manage to garner a repeat airing the following year. And, as we've established, Stilgoe was fresh in the memories of the intended audience. So this poses a pertinent question: is this lack of recall indicative of the programme's quality?

Stilgoe is central to the show. He's an enthusiastic host and flits from table to table without ever losing interest. His innate knack for knocking up ridiculously catchy songs is also pushed to the fore. The theme tune is an infectious earworm and the tunetastic action doesn't stop here. There are also fantastically silly songs to be enjoyed such as Bearobics and Vegetables Ain't People.

And the musical elements are complemented by a varied range of guests. They have little to do with relieving boredom, but they do bring a bit of a variety feel to *Stilgoe's On.* While not as exciting as pop stars, there's a generous dose of magic behind puppeteers and ventriloquists. They're very traditional forms of entertainment and keep the episodes ticking along.

The activities being offered up to counter boredom will be familiar, in one form or another, to anyone who grew up in the pre-internet age. The series brings to mind rainy afternoons spent in primary school. Or, those wonderful days, when a supply teacher came to school and completely disregarded the curriculum. There may be little to excite the senses in these sections, but it's harmless fare.

Although *Stilgoe's On* doesn't offer up anything revolutionary in terms of occupying a child's mind, it's not without merit. The main takeaway from the show is that it underlines the importance of a DIY approach to entertainment. Designing an imaginary town with coloured paper and sticky tape may seem frivolous, but its real purpose is to fire creativity when faced with scant resources. A gentle and nostalgic treat.

TREASURES OF THE MINDLORD

ITV
1986

There was relatively little for children to do once the school bell had rung in 1986. The main options were: struggle with fiendishly difficult homework, get up to all sorts of trouble over at the local park and, most honourable, catch a couple of hours' worth of children's television.

However, if you were fortuitous, there was another option. A very exciting option. Excitement tends to be a subjective concept, but the thrill of tackling an intergalactic Mindlord and securing the future of Earth is unarguable. It certainly beats anything set by a French teacher. And, most exciting of all, there was the chance to win the *Treasures of the Mindlord*.

Enyon (Richard Worthy) is the Mindlord of a thousand stars and he's most intrigued by the culture of Earth. Despite Earth's culture being young, Enyon can see that it is advancing rapidly. And he is open to the Earthlings joining his confederation. First, though, they must prove their suitability. In order to avoid the wrath of Enyon, the Earthlings must combine all their wit, guile and steel to complete a cycle of tests. If they succeed then they are rewarded with a place in Enyon's galactic confederation. And win £300 for their school to spend on computer equipment.

The two teams of two school children begin their quests by being beamed – via transmortagraphs – onto a space pod with two of Enyon's subordinates. Jana (Kate Newell) – all clad in blue and sporting a gold headscarf – acts as a guide for the

121

Earth children and helps to explain the challenges ahead. Kerna (Steve Cooke) is a computer who can multitask with the best of them; he keeps a note of the scores, sets questions and, most dramatically, plucks the contestants in and out of time tunnels.

The labyrinth of tests and tricks begins with one of the teams being placed in a time tunnel whilst the other prepares to run Enyon's gauntlet. One of the contestants remains on the pod with Jana and Kerna and, from here, they guide their fellow team member. This counterpart has, by now, been beamed down to an Earth location such as an ancient country manor or a power plant. Here they must make their way through dark, smoky corridors as their team mate relays instructions and riddles provided by Kerna.

But they're not alone. In amongst the dark are two more of Enyon's minions. The Wizard (Jeremy Curry) and the dwarf To-Lar (Mike Edmonds) are bumbling souls, but they come packed with general knowledge questions which must be answered in order to win credits. It should also be pointed out that, every few minutes, the competing team is put into a time tunnel by Kerna to allow the other team to compete. Following these initial rounds it's time for the contestants to move onto more interactive sections.

First off, it's time for the contestants to take seat in an ancient chair where they are set three questions. However, time is of the essence. A computer animation is simultaneously playing out which features threats such as Martian microbes or the Death Head of Trygon Nebulas advancing on the contestant. Directly after this, the contestants must enter an area where they search for treasures, including a gold walnut and a queen's locket, and place them on an illuminated table.

Each treasure is assigned a score and the aim is to scavenge as many of them as possible to boost the teams' final scores.

Both teams are then reunited on the space pod with Jana and Kerna to evaluate the scores. The team with the most credits is granted the chance to search for Enyon and face his ultimate challenge. Jana enters a code into Kerna and the forcefield is deactivated. The exploring contestant is then sent back to Earth where they must seek out a final location code. And it's this location code which will guide them towards Enyon, who has one last question to pose.

The glittering contents of *Treasures of the Mindlord* was devised by David R Scott and David Drewery with their idea put into production by Television South West. Seven episodes, which ran to around 25 minutes each, slotted into the Children's ITV schedule of 1986 and occupied the 4.20pm slot. Publicity for the series was scarce. Aside from a short feature in the TV Times there was very little press coverage. The feature from the TV Times also makes reference to the show winning a silver plaque at a Canadian children's TV festival. Sadly, the identity of this festival has been lost to the sands of time.

There are television shows which barely get a mention when it comes to reminiscing about childhood viewing. Likewise, there are television shows that, it would appear, you and only you remember. And then there is *Treasures of the Mindlord*. To say that it's an obscurity of children's television is an understatement. *Treasures of the Mindlord* is barely a blip on the register of British television history. Most people would rather not discuss show a show. But you, dear reader, are different. You live for the ephemera of British television. And, who knows, maybe you even remember *Treasures of the Mindlord.*

To discuss *Treasures of the Mindlord*, though, requires us to acknowledge the elephant in the room. Identifying said elephant should be an open and shut case. Remotely guided teams? Computer graphics? And wizards? This elephant can only be *Knightmare*. And, truly, *Knightmare* was one of the finest children's television ever produced. Running for seven series, the quests of Treguard carved their way into the consciousness of a generation. *Treasures of the Mindlord* fails spectacularly in matching this. Nonetheless, it managed to bring the concept to our screens a whole year before *Knightmare* did.

The head start provided by its earlier transmission date does two things: it removes any accusations of plagiarism and it marks *Treasures of the Mindlord* out as an innovative example of children's programming. Shades of *The Adventure Game* colour the series, but it's a very different show. A contrast highlighted by the extensive location filming and the race against Enyon's clock. It's an immersive experience and, while it may feel unsophisticated in its execution, its scope has to be admired.

The cast may, aside from Mike Edmonds, be unfamiliar to most, but they inhabit their roles with an admirable enthusiasm. And this is all the more remarkable given the rather flat scripts that they are equipped with. Nonetheless, the dialogue does little to take the shine off the performances. And Richard Worthy should be applauded for channelling Enyon with such an authoritative menace.

The contestants are, as you would imagine, the usual procession of 1980s haircuts and NHS prescription glasses (hey, we've all been there). But, dated fashions aside, the contestants are there to work as a team. And *Treasures of the Mindlord* demands team work. There's no room for dead wood whether it's answering general knowledge questions about Wham! or guiding their mate through the various locations. And the production should be praised for concentrating its efforts on this commendable quality.

Where *Treasures of the Mindlord* struggles to shine is its propensity for repetition. Both teams follow the exact same routes and, for the viewer, it soon becomes an exercise in thumb twiddling. The show is also guilty of having a rather ramshackle feel. This is no surprise given the 'real time' nature of the quests and location filming, but an all-enveloping atmosphere fails to descend.

One of the real bugbears, for the contestants at least, is the prizes on offer. Winning computer vouchers is fantastic for your school, yet, for the contestant, it counts for little when they head home. And, regardless of whether you're on the winning or losing team, *everyone* wins a personal stereo. Sure, it's a nice prize for 1986, but a lack of prize tiers does little to inspire motivation.

The heartbeat of *Treasures of the Mindlord* is one which has failed to echo into the 21st century. The demise of the programme resulted in few mourners and even they have long since forgotten about it. Be that as it may, with a little tinkering it could have ironed out *some* of its problems. Nevertheless, the *Knightmare* factor would have remained. A much slicker and advanced programme, *Knightmare* was iconic television.

It's unlikely that *Treasures of the Mindlord*, with its already dated BBC Micro graphics, would have stood a chance on the same channel. But there's a curious swashbuckling charm at the heart of the series. And, most admirably, *Treasures of the Mindlord* manages to tread an intriguing and innovative path all of its own. Even if you can't remember it, you need to try and track an episode down. It may leave you scratching your head at times, but *Treasures of the Mindlord* is far from forgettable.

PINNY'S HOUSE

BBC1
1986

Childhood brings a number of vertical challenges. And these can be highly frustrating. Especially when you want to see what all the adults are peering at out of the window. Time, thankfully, reduces this frustration as our gradual accumulation of inches grants us enhanced viewing capabilities. This makes life much easier. But not everyone is privy to the wonders of growth. If you're a tiny doll then you're fixed in a permanent state of smallness. And this can lead to a hair-raising adventure around every corner as seen in *Pinny's House*.

Victor is the smallest wooden sailor in the world. And, despite this record breaking fact, he lives upon a humble shelf in his blue, wooden sailing ship. Next door to Victor, on said shelf, is an empty china house which is briefly home to a green beetle and a web-spinning spider. It's a fairly lonely existence for Victor despite the regular attentions of two young children: Jo and Tom. However, things are about to change for Victor.

One day, whilst playing in the sitting room, Jo places a pedlar doll up on the shelf next to Victor. In amongst the wares of this pedlar doll, Victor spies a wooden doll named Pinny. The pedlar doll is a keen businesswoman and demands payment for Pinny. After scrambling round in the dust and fluff of the sitting room floor, Victor finds an old ring which he exchanges for Pinny.

Pinny, after chasing off the green beetle and the spider, takes up residence in the china house. This, of course, isn't the end of the story. Instead there are a plethora of adventures lying ahead for Pinny and Victor.

A particularly harrowing jaunt for Pinny finds her being blown outside by a strong gust of wind. Here she finds herself mistaken for a twig by a thrush keen on building a nest. Victor, meanwhile, suffers the ignominy of being sucked up by a vacuum cleaner and discarded into a bin bag. And, perhaps most dangerously, a trip to the beach almost leads to Pinny and Victor being swept out to sea.

Pinny's House was written by Peter Firmin with his longstanding colleague Oliver Postgate acting as producer. 13 episodes were produced for Children's BBC with the series' run beginning in October 1986 in a 3.55pm slot. Episodes were repeated across BBC1 and BBC2 for several years; the final transmission of *Pinny's House* came in May 1993.

Matilda Thorpe, who had recently appeared in ITV's *Words, Words, Words,* describes her involvement in *Pinny's House:*

"It was one of my first jobs after leaving drama school and it wasn't a very high profile audition. I think it was between myself and one other. We both went to a studio and recorded some lines, a short while afterwards I got a call from my agent saying they would like me to do it. I was told to take a particular train down to the recording studios in Kent and that it would take a full day to record. And I was sent all the books and scripts ahead of time to practise. The job was very important to me as I had never recorded long narration before. Lots to think about – not to let your energy drop, keep the sound fresh and motivated and to tell the story as if the viewer was sitting next to you"

And working with Postgate and Firmin proved to be a

fantastic experience for Thorpe:

"They were two of the giants of animation in this country. I had grown up watching Ivor the Engine, Pogles Wood, The Clangers and Bagpuss. The pair of them were both very low key, charming, hardworking and focussed. I was quite young and not brave enough to ask questions about their other work. They were humble and very involved in their work. Not at all starry"

Little introduction is needed for Oliver Postgate and Peter Firmin. They were the masters of capturing the fickle attention spans of children and engaging them for decades afterwards. It would be far from hyperbole to describe them as gods of British children's TV. And, although *Pinny's House* was the final production by Smallfilms, they remained dedicated to the very end of their animated empire.

Victor and Pinny regularly find themselves hurtling towards danger and it's usually through no fault of their own. And this is a reflection of the situation the young viewers would find themselves in. The world is an unpredictable place when you're three, so security is a crucial commodity. The problem with security is that too much is detrimental to a child's development. That's not to say that all boundaries are off, but, you know, children need to experience life to some degree. Postgate understands this and infuses *Pinny's House* with some vital life lessons.

A common device in *Pinny's House* is for Victor and Pinny to find themselves outside and far away from the comfort of their shelf. This displacement is conjured up in a number of ways unlikely to affect a small child – such as falling deep within a floppy, cloth frog and being carried outside by a dog. But the basic premise of separation anxiety is something which taps into the mindset of all children.

Children's TV isn't there to be a discourse on the realities of life and helplessness, so *Pinny's House* eschews any truly harrowing concepts. Instead, Firmin's stories lend a helping hand to children. And he does this through the bravery and initiative displayed by Victor and Pinny. Taking a feather from a bird's nest that she's trapped in, Pinny manages to float down to the safety Victor's boat. Likewise, another episode finds Victor stranded on the sitting room floor. Disaster is avoided, though, when Pinny engages the services of a toy truck to help hoist Victor back up to the shelf.

When it comes to the production side of things, it's business as usual for Smallfilms. Pinny and Victor are hardly rendered with an exceptional amount of detail, but the child friendly illustrations create a world that's easy to engage with. Equally important is the calming, serene narration provided by Matilda Thorpe. She grants a motherly charm to proceedings which is protective and reassuring. Perhaps most underrated, is the contribution of Ar Log. Their battling accordions, woodwinds and strings provide an enchanting folk soundtrack which encapsulates the action on the screen.

Each episode of *Pinny's House* ends with either Jo or Tom remarking that "Something terrible might have happened" But there's never any chance of this happening in view of Pinny and Victor's intelligence. The two dolls certainly don't have the aspirational qualities of superheroes, but they're not here to save the world from galactic villains.

Pinny and Victor are here to guide young children through

those tentative first steps in a world which, even as an adult, feels baffling at the best of times. And it's all captured by the time honoured traditions of Smallfilms production techniques. Although *Pinny's House* may appear to be a slight series of adventures, it conceals a beautiful brand of untold magic.

C.A.B

ITV
1986 – 1989

Since its inception in 1939, the Citizens Advice Bureau has helped millions of Brits. Its success has been remarkable and it remains a trusted dispenser of advice. Indirectly, it has also helped to establish a sibling-based succession of secret agents for whom espionage is their raison d'être. You may wonder how the Citizens Advice Bureau can go from legal wrangles over land ownership to thwarting the theft of Tutunkhamun's treasure, but there is truth to this madness. If you want to find out more then you'll need to get in contact with *C.A.B.*

Colin Freshwater (Felipe Izquierdo) has aspirations of becoming a secret agent. Unfortunately he's a little lacking in certain departments. For one thing he doesn't have a codename. And neither does he have a way of recording his findings. That's all about to change thanks to junk shop owner Ma Mossop (Avril Angers).

The junk shop was originally a branch of the Citizen's Advice Bureau and the shop window still bears their name, so Colin takes their initials to become secret agent C.A.B. Ma Mossop enhances his credentials further by providing him with a dictaphone on which he can record his adventures. But this is where Ma Mossop's direct encouragement will stop. She's heading into hospital, so this means she needs someone to look after Tatters the cat. And this task falls to Colin and his reluctant sidekick Franny Barnes (Louise Mason).

Looking after Tatters is straightforward. It's the rest that will test Colin and Franny. A procession of shady characters soon visit the shop and include the 'master' of disguise Smith (Graham Seed), duplicitous toad and schemer Hellman (Frank Gatliff) and the enigmatic Egyptian Anwar (Lyndam Gregory). All three have a vested interest in the true location of Tutankhamun's treasure. And it's down to Colin and Franny to thwart them by solving hieroglyphic riddles and protecting a valuable map.

By the start of the second series, Ma Mossop has relocated to Eel Pie Island. Her shop, now run by Hellman, has moved across town where it operates as a travel agents called The Wooden Kamel. Rather than selling package tours to the Costa del Sol, The Wooden Kamel is as ingrained with mystery as ever. A mysterious sarcophagus stands proudly in the shop. A set of menacing blue eyes glow brightly from an ancient cat statue. And a trainer wearing policeman (David Janes) is lurking upstairs in a hidden room.

The third, and final, series ushers in a number of changes. Franny, who pops up briefly in the first episode, is no longer part of the action, but Colin is not alone. He's now joined by his little brother Jace (Ben Felton) and Franny's younger sister Tracey (Tracey McDonald). There's also help from an enigmatic plumber by the name of Vine (Michael Bertenshaw). Together, they must take on Eleanor Plantagenet (Judith Paris) who hopes to seize the throne of England through the power of the mythical Queen's Beast.

C.A.B's cryptic exploits started life in 1986 as a Thames Television production for Children's ITV. However, the production did not get off to the best of starts. Denise Coffey, as she revealed to fan site C.A.B HQ (cabhq.50webs.com), did not start writing the series, but found herself rushed into completing the scripts as an emergency replacement. In spite of this, with the storyline already planned, Coffey was able to pen the rest of the episodes with relative ease. Coffey only worked on the first series and, for *C.A.B's* second and third outings, Thames stalwart John Kershaw took charge of the scripts.

Despite three series airing in quick succession, and comprising 33 episodes, *C.A.B* remains an irretrievable memory for most of those watching children's TV in the mid to late 1980s. And this is a perplexing situation as *C.A.B* contains many bizarre and hallucinogenic moments. Colin suffers ominous, haunting visions of a mysterious sarcophagus throughout the first series and the second contains a surreal sequence where a miniature Hellman skips next to Colin's bed with a hypnotic rhythm. But this all pales into insignificance next to the denouement of the third series.

It's a sequence so disturbing that it gives *Children of the Stones* a run for its money. And it's a rare show that can make such claims. Yet, with Eleanor Plantagenet's face burning and cracking apart amidst a psychedelic light show, *C.A.B* more than holds its own. Combined with the sound of thunder, screaming and otherworldly noises, it's one of the strangest scenes ever transmitted. Quite how this moment wasn't indelibly burned onto the retinas of a generation is mystifying.

But, while these bizarre moments are visually very impressive, you soon get the impression that *C.A.B* is a little too mind-bending. Nearly every aspect of the plot seems determined to morph from one conundrum to another. And the resultant mystery permeates every pore of the narrative. Logic becomes a loose concept and keeping track of the action soon becomes an uphill task.

Nonetheless, all three series benefit from unique storylines which embrace mythical centrepieces and a mature brand of villainy. The espionage angle of the series drives the excitement upwards as do the high levels of peril that await our young special agents. And these aspects are strengthened further by the performances.

Felipe Izquierdo and Louise Mason both give confident performances throughout *C.A.B*, but it appears that a career in acting evaded them both. Mason disappeared shortly after *C.A.B* whilst Izquierdo fared only slightly better with several credits up until the late 1990s. The adults, blessed with experience, summon up the best performances in *C.A.B*. Frank Gatliff is the jewel in the crown with his portrayal of the treacherous, snivelling Hellman a real highlight. And Judith Paris' wilfully bonkers turn as Eleanor Plantagent is a powerful and menacing performance.

C.A.B isn't the most obscure piece of children's programming in this book, but its legacy is certainly shrouded in dust and uncertainty. Maybe it reached a little too far in its quest for mystery and baffled viewers in a way that its contemporaries avoided. In spite of this, *C.A.B* is far from a late afternoon folly. It has its flaws, but there's nothing more intriguing than a flawed triumph.

SWINGS AND ROUNDABOUTS

ITV
1987 to 1989

The British Isles display a wealth of idiosyncrasies in every corner that you care to crane your neck into. These characteristics are varied and can take in geography, social practices and history. While it's important that we understand these variances on a national level, it's crucial that we focus on those that affect us locally.

Interpreting the vicinity around us allows us to navigate it. And for British children, who spend most of their small lives stranded on an island, this is doubly important. A criticism of British television, however, is that it tends to concentrate on life in England. Thankfully, the wonders of regional programming provide an alternative. And, for children in Northern Ireland, this local knowledge can be found in *Swings and Roundabouts*.

Jane Cassidy is on a mission to educate the children of Northern Ireland about the sights and sounds around them. First and foremost, Jane Cassidy is a singer, so you can also expect a wealth of Ulster folk music. But the programme is about more than Cassidy singing songs about the animals of Dublin Zoo (yes, she sometimes strays into the Republic too). Whilst the folk songs bookend the episodes, the main content takes an all-encompassing look at life in Northern Ireland. And Jane isn't on her own. She's joined by Barney, a round orange ball-shaped character who measures roughly a foot high.

Together, Jane and Barney travel all over Northern Ireland

investigating a series of unique locations. A trip to Lough Neagh looks at life for the local fisherman and the accompanying population of two-million eels. Jane and Barney take a trip back through time at the Ulster American Folk Park in County Tyrone. And there's also time for our presenting duo to head over to Belfast to see how a newspaper is put together.

Swings and Roundabouts was made for the children of Northern Ireland and, on the whole, was only seen by the children of Northern Ireland. The series was produced by Ulster TV and ran as a Northern Ireland opt-out section of the ITV Schools schedule. The occasional scheduling conflict, however, ensured that, from time to time, the series appeared on the entire ITV network.

Regardless of where *Swings and Roundabouts* aired, it stuck to the usual parameters of ITV Schools programming; the episodes, which aired between 1987 and 1989, ran for between 10 – 15 minutes each. An initial pilot for the show was recorded in 1986 and is most notable for reducing Barney's design to that of a glove puppet.

The rather diminutive landmass of Great Britain could easily lead to an outsider deducing that any variations are minimal. But they couldn't be more wrong. Accents, social practices, foods, legalities and manufacturing processes: they're radically different from region to region. And *Swings and Roundabouts* strives to underline the diversities of Northern Ireland. Pride certainly cometh before a fall, but the pride that *Swings and Roundabouts* instils is of a more honourable variety. Whether it's blowing glass in County Tyrone or exploring the Marble Arch Caves, it's all about celebrating the country's rich culture.

As part of the ITV Schools schedule it is, naturally,

educative. Although it's a strain of learning that is far from gruelling; *Swings and Roundabouts* is much more in keeping with a lunchtime children's show. There's no heavy repetition and no follow up questions to tax the mind. And the friendly, approachable nature of the learning is reflected in Jane Cassidy. With a personality that is simultaneously cheery, eager and amiable, Cassidy is the embodiment of everything that education should be about.

Swings and Roundabouts may appear to be simple programming, but this is what makes it successful. The diversity of Britain is so strong that even tackling a small landmass such as Northern Ireland is a big ask. Yet *Swings and Roundabouts* sets out its stall by concentrating on the more digestible aspects of each topic. And it easily fulfils its objective of establishing the importance of a local identity.

KELLYVISION

ITV
1988

It's likely, given that you're reading this book, that you have more than a passing interest in television. And television, particularly British television, is magnificent. But are we aware of just how much hard work goes into producing it? The truth is that, as we sit gorging ourselves on the finest culture ever transmitted, we barely give a second thought to the blood, sweat and tears invested by the production team. Thankfully, there's hope for those of us who want to hoover up every single morsel of information relating to television production. And this hope comes in the form of *Kellyvision*.

The television programmes we see on our screens are, mostly, slick affairs. Yet this level of professionalism is far from effortless. It takes hard work, multiple takes and endless stress. Perfectly poised to appreciate these processes are presenters Chris Kelly and Gaz Top. Venturing out in the wide and varied world of television, Kelly and Top will undertake a comprehensive look at how television programmes are put together. Each episode of *Kellyvision* concentrates on a specific production technique and then drills deep down into its core.

The magic of bluescreen technology is highlighted by the cutting-edge graphics of *Knightmare*. The mammoth team (and endless equipment) involved in outside broadcasts is put under the microscope at ITV Sports. And time is even allocated to finding out what it's like to work with the PG Chimps on commercials.

Nine episodes of *Kellyvision* were produced by Tyne Tees Television for Children's ITV. The episodes ran to 20 minutes each and went out on Wednesday afternoons at 4.50pm. *Kellyvision* remained a single series production and was not lucky enough to garner any repeat showings. It did, however, lead to a one-off special featuring Gaz Top in 1989 titled *Movie Magic: Erik the Viking.*

Gareth Jones – aka Gaz Top – was relatively new to television at the time, but his face was still familiar to viewers as he reveals:

"From 1986 I had been working on Get Fresh, a live Saturday morning series that was made by a different ITV company every week, but the central unit, the production core as it were, was run by Tyne-Tees TV who had pitched Kellyvision to Children's ITV. And, because of my existing relationship with Tyne-Tees, I was in their roster of presenters who were known to children. The producer of Kellyvision Lesley Oakden had worked on an episode of Get Fresh and I suppose it was her who considered me as a possible co-presenter with Chris Kelly"

Not content with being one of the faces of *Kellyvision*, Jones also stepped up when it came to creating the series' theme tune:

"I was in a band at the time, called "The Tuphelo Torpedoes" with my pal Steve Allan Jones. We had song ideas a-plenty and it seemed a logical step to offer our skills to the production. I recorded a rough demo on cassette at home in my flat in north London, then got the go-ahead from Lesley Oakden to record it properly, so we went to a small studio in a bloke's house somewhere in west London and recorded the tune. I sang the vocal line and played the guitar. Steve Allan, probably the best musician I

know, programmed the drums and keyboard track and provided the speaking parts. Later we also recorded the title music for a series I appeared on made by Grampian TV called Video Jukebox"

Jones also reveals that there was one episode of *Kellyvision* which, for understandable reasons, never made it to the airwaves:

"There was one episode of Kellyvision that we recorded that was never broadcast. It was a programme about guns and explosions in film and television, it dealt with pyrotechnics and how actors are trained to handle weapons and fire blanks. In-between the programme being edited and broadcast a gunman shot and killed 16 people in Hungerford. Therefore, quite rightly, ITV took the decision that the content of this episode of Kellyvision was now too sensitive and so the edition was never transmitted"

From 1972 through to 1981 Chris Kelly presented *Clapperboard,* a masterful children's series which took an exhaustive look at the world of film and cinema. It was an insightful programme and one that demonstrated a strong respect for the young viewers' intelligence. *Kellyvision* is no different.

The levels of enthusiasm on offer are exceptional and the refusal to talk down to children is resolute. Few programmes can boast such accolades and Chris Kelly is lucky enough to have featured in two of them. But, as with *Clapperboard,* it's the nuances and level of detail available that make *Kellyvision* stand out. Young viewers would be hard pushed to find this content elsewhere.

Puppets, for example, are a mainstay of children's television, yet how many children know how these programmes end up on the screen? Very few. But *Kellyvision* is on hand to rectify this with an episode that focuses on the production of *Spitting Image*. And it covers an entire episode from start to finish. So, we get to see how the scenery is built, the voice work recorded and, finally, how the programme is transmitted to the nation.

There's also time to underline the frantic work involved in putting together a weekly pop show. And, to achieve this, *Kellyvision* takes a short walk across the Tyne Tees production lot to visit *The Roxy*. This episode is an exercise in the importance of precision in television and finds time to showcase the lyrical skills of Bomb the Bass. It's also notable for a scene where both Top's and Pat Sharpe's gravity-defying mullets are on screen at the same time.

The content on tap is educative, although never overbearing. There's just enough depth available. It reels you in and never repels you with a tedious list of weighty terminology. And that's what keeps the viewer on board. Time is also of the essence and the 20-minute episodes make for lively, sprightly affairs. And there's a striking dichotomy between the two presenters Kelly was plucked from the womb with bags of old school charm. And he dispenses it here with an untold generosity. Top, meanwhile, is equally enthusiastic. But he brings a much more modern brand of excitement and engagement.

Despite being restricted to a children's slot, *Kellyvision* is more than capable of holding its own with an adult audience. Even three decades on, despite many of the production techniques now being outdated, the episodes remain fascinating insights into the craft of making television. It *could* be argued that *Kellyvision* removes a little of the magic behind television.

However, this would be a pompous stance to take. If anything, *Kellyvision* enhances the enjoyment of television by affording the viewer a new perspective on their favourite shows.

There's just one drawback when it comes to *Kellyvision*: only nine episodes were made; the number of subjects that *could* have been covered is almost infinite. Rather than grousing about this 30 years on, though, it's much simpler to revel in these nine amazing episodes and celebrate the art of television.

MOONDIAL

BBC1
1988

Teenage life, even at the best of times, can be a complicated and troublesome affair. The many stressors and demands placed upon a developing mind can create great stress and confusion. Thankfully, teenagers are hardy souls. And they always emerge from these experiences as stronger individuals.

But it's not always this easy. Events can sometimes spiral out of control during pubescence. Family tragedy, for example, can magnify a teenager's mental fog to extreme levels. And when you *also* have to deal with evil, time travelling ghost hunters it's a bona fide nightmare. It's also the basis for *Moondial.*

Following the death of her father, Minty (Siri Neal) has been out of sorts and her mother (Joanna Dunham) decides that a change of scenery may help. Minty soon finds herself travelling to Lincolnshire to live with her Aunt Mary (Valerie Lush). For Minty, though, the tranquil change of surroundings fails to instil much calm. Minty's fragile state of mind immediately takes a knock when her mother is involved in a car crash. In between visits to her comatose mother in hospital, Minty attempts to find some sense of normality at Aunt Mary's. But matters in Lincolnshire appear to be far from normal.

Labelled as an outcast by the local children, Minty seeks refuge in the beautiful grounds of Belton House. And it's here that Minty finds herself drawn towards a mysterious moondial. Flanked by statues of Chronos and Eros, this curious moondial is more than just a standard timepiece. It's capable of transporting Minty back in time.

Minty's first travels take her back to the Victorian era where she meets the kitchen boy, Tom (Tony Sands). Despite suffering from a nasty case of tuberculosis, Tom exhibits a guttersnipe charm and befriends Minty with ease. Eventually, the power of the moondial drags them further back in time to the 18th century. And it's here that they encounter the troubled Sarah (Helena Avellano).

Blighted by a birthmark which her contemporaries believe is the mark of the devil, Sarah leads a lonely and terrified existence. In order to protect the wider world from her satanic corruption, Sarah is hidden away deep within Belton House. Yet Sarah is not alone. She is presided over by the seething cruelty of Miss Vole (Jacqueline Pearce).

Determined to save both Sarah and Tom from their cheerless existences, Minty sets out to bring peace to their lives. She may have a plan for the past, but Minty still needs to deal with the present; the stress of her mother's condition continues to eat away at her. And there's one final hurdle in the modern day. A curiously familiar ghost hunter has arrived in the form of Miss Raven (Jacqueline Pearce).

The spooky stylings of *Moondial* first appeared on the screens of unsuspecting viewers in 1988. The programme was a BBC production and was based on Helen Cresswell's 1987 novel of the same name. The six episodes of *Moondial* made their home in the 5.10pm slot of the Children's BBC schedule on Wednesdays. A repeat transmission for *Moondial* came two years later in 1990.

Colin Cant, a historic figure for being the first director of

Grange Hill, directed *Moondial* and would later go on to direct the equally mysterious serials *Dark Season* and *Century Falls.* Tony Sands remembers Cant being the perfect director as he digs through his memories of *Moondial:*

"I trained at The Anna Scher children's Theatre in Islington, North London and was put forward to audition for the series. I was very fortunate and Colin Cant, the director, gave me an opportunity. Colin was great to work with. It's weird now, looking at his body of work and realising just how good he was at his job. He made it look quite effortless really. A nice man.

The cast all got on well, on set and off. Siri and I used to practice lines together in the evenings. We had a great crew, really friendly people who made the whole experience easy and enjoyable. And Jacqueline Pearce, well, I loved Blake's Seven so I recognised her as soon as I saw her. Someone told me not to mention it, but I couldn't help myself and told her I loved the show. She burst out into a huge smile"

The on-set atmosphere may have been convivial, but the atmosphere onscreen is terrifying. And *Moondial* starts with a cold opening which is one of the most chilling things ever seen on British television. If it were purely an auditory experience then the ominous, rumbling organs and shrieking, ghostly wails would be nightmarish enough. However, this is television. And this means there are also visuals.

As the unearthly symphony unfolds, a young girl in white sets off from a set of church gates, making her way across a moonlit lawn and towards a moondial where she pauses. A light in a grand house at the top of the lawn draws her attention and she hurries towards it. Peering into the window, she's confronted by a ghostly apparition of herself being pursued by a lady in black who wrestles her away screaming.

The disconcerting visuals don't stop here and Colin Cant's direction delights in testing the hairs on the back of your neck. A gang of rowdy and bloodthirsty children beat and burn a mannequin said to represent Sarah. Tom coughs up a lungful of blood in a particularly grisly scene. And, later, Sarah is confronted by a young, baying mob all clad in terrifying masks.

Clearly, the visuals in *Moondial* are strong and sinister, but what of the story? A talented, and much loved writer, Helen Cresswell has crafted something quite terrific with *Moondial*. It stands apart from the rest of her writing and underlines the range she had at her disposal. Taking in the concepts of time travel and the supernatural, *Moondial* has strong foundations for creating a special tale.

And the end result is a narrative which confounds and excites at every turn. It helps that there's a brand of penetrating horror at play. *Moondial,* though, is about much more than psychological scares. It's also an exercise in the power of altruism. Despite the crushing sense of angst infecting her own life, Minty demonstrates great selflessness in coming to Tom and Sarah's aidd.

Where *Moondial* falters slightly is its liberal spreading of mystery throughout the series. Certain aspects feel under explained such as the origins of the moondial's power. And where do the ghostly children go skipping off to at the end? Was it even real in the first place? But perhaps it's a little unfair to dwell on these aspects too much. Even the finest scripts require a certain suspension of disbelief.

One area which doesn't require any criticism is the acting.

Minty's determined strength is channelled confidently by Siri Neal in one of the earliest roles of her short career. And she manages to strike up a fantastic 'odd couple' chemistry with the Dickensian sensibilities of Tony Sand's Tom. Less prevalent, in terms of dialogue, Helena Avellano has considerably little to do compared to her peers. At the very least, though, she cuts a harried figure well.

The final seal of quality comes in the performance of Jacqueline Pearce. An expert in intensity, Pearce conjures up a an unhinged glamour mixed with psychopathy in both her roles. Miss Vole contains an intense and burning terror which is capable of inducing goosebumps at 40 paces. And Miss Raven, while more discreet, brings a glint of malevolent evil with each flash of her dark, dangerous eyes.

Moondial is a multi-layered tale that takes in displacement, malicious forces and a generous side order of angst. And there are few children's shows which can boast such a combination. The series may occasionally fall short in the logic stakes, but it more than makes up for this in its eerie, visual magnificence. And, once watched, *Moondial* is never forgotten.

WINDFALLS

ITV
1989

We're so busy rushing about that we're constantly looking ahead and worrying what's coming towards us. Sure, it's an invaluable skill to possess whilst driving. And it's crucial for navigating your way through the Boxing Day sales. But there's a whole world beneath our feet. So it's a shame that we miss out on the wonders below. And, if you were to cock your eye towards the grass and leaves, you might be lucky enough to glimpse some *Windfalls*.

"Wherever there are flowers and trees and grass there's always a Windfall Land. And in every Windfall Land you'll find Windfalls" narrator Peter Hawkins informs us as *Windfalls* starts, but what are Windfalls? Well, they're little characters made up from the leaves, petals and grasses that make up the natural landscape of Windfall Land. The main focus of *Windfalls* centres upon three of the Windfalls: Berry, Butterbur and Rosebay.

Together, these three characters interact with the many other inhabitants of Windfall Land such as Uncle Onion, Bella Donna, Cornflower and Evening Primrose. And what sort of adventures could be awaiting such an unusual collection of characters? *Windfalls* is set in the world of nature and is comprised from nature's own materials. This is where *Windfalls* takes its cue from. Ever wondered how a rainbow forms? The Windfalls are on hand to explain. Ever wondered how dock leaves can nullify a sting? Just ask the Windfalls. And ever wondered about the dangers of eating wild berries? Well, you get the idea.

Created and written by actress, writer and traditional cooking expert Jenny Kenna, *Windfalls* consisted of 26 episodes. The series was produced by Central TV and FilmFair with episodes going out in the Friday 4.05pm slot on Children's ITV. Kenna reveals that the inspiration for *Windfalls* was one that was close to her heart and this passion helped her get the show onto our screens:

"My love of flowers and nature in general was my original inspiration. I began to press flowers and leaves to create colourful collages of floral arrangements and one day by pure chance I formed a floral character. Before long I had a whole array of characters and knew they had to be part of a story and the natural story-lines could only be those linked to nature truths of which there were many. Whilst writing these stories I met a TV producer who suggested the concept would make an interesting children's television series.

I was introduced to Graham Clutterbuck of FilmFair and was told that if I could get my characters to walk across the screen they would consider making a pilot which would then be shown to Central TV in the hope that a series would be commissioned. Graham provided me with a small studio, a rostrum camera and a month to experiment. It was very daunting but I was determined to get my little characters (which were only a few inches high) to walk. At the end of the month this was achieved albeit in very jerky fashion. Graham was delighted and soon an experienced animation team were brought together"

Although a second series never followed - tragically, Graham Clutterbuck died before the end of the series - and repeats were not forthcoming, 18 of the 26 episodes were released over three VHS releases through the Little Croft Studios label.

What's most immediately striking about *Windfalls* is its unusual aesthetics. The use of natural materials used to shape Windfall Land ensures that it looks unlike any of its contemporaries. *Windfalls* is heavily indebted to nature and, as a result, feels much more like a European folk tale produced on the continent rather than at home in Britain.

The unique look taps perfectly into the ethos of the series, but working with all those organic materials must have been a nightmare, right? Well, Jenny Kenna remembers it being testing, yet more than achievable with the right amount of skill and care:

"The natural materials were obviously very fragile so delicate handling was essential. Fortunately, my clever French animator Isobel Perrichon was very dexterous, she hardly ever mislaid or damaged a single fragment including the lips, as these were made from miniscule pieces of petals and the eyes in many cases were tiny forget-me-not flowers. All the work had to be done using watchmakers tweezers from assembling the characters and backgrounds to the actual animation itself. Animation with real flowers, leaves and grasses had never been done before so it did take a bit of practice to get used to working with this medium but once achieved the job became easier"

And, of course, the whole production had the backing and talents of FilmFair to call upon. With their inimitable magic on tap, FilmFair bring an added layer of charm to *Windfalls*. Working with FilmFair and, in particular, Graham Clutterbuck was a fantastic experience for Kenna as she reveals:

"FilmFair would not have been FilmFair without Graham Clutterbuck. He had the gift of understanding children's mentality and knowing instinctively what type of programmes they would love to watch. It was a pleasure to go to work each day and to be surrounded by so many creative people.

The whole atmosphere at Jacob's Well Mews was thrilling - perhaps Paddington Bear was being edited in one of the editing suites or the rushes of Portland Bill were being viewed in another. It was a hub of creativity and I felt very privileged to be part of it all and proud that I played a small part of the animation life at FilmFair"

Windfalls is, of course, a show for children, so how does it fare in that respect? Well, Jenny Kenna is not alone in her love of nature. Children are obsessed with it; who doesn't remember the excitement of poking around in bushes, throwing leaves up in the air or closely examining the wonder of a fallen acorn? And this sense of wonder is at the very heart of *Windfalls*. Each and every scene is an engaging adventure into the natural beauty of our surroundings.

There's also a concerted effort to combine learning with these beautiful aesthetics. The adventures awaiting our floral friends are far from exhilarating, rollercoaster rides, but their placid approach helps to gently underline the learning. The extensive realm of flora is rarely covered in children's TV and *Windfalls* is to be congratulated for this. Organic television at its finest.

CHRIS AND CRUMBLE

BBC2
1989

A universal fear for children is that there's a monster lurking under their bed. It may seem irrational to adults, but there's substance to this concern. Beds are warm, secure places and a child *should* feel safe to lay there for several hours in a state of deep sleep. The obstacle to this security lies underneath the bed.

Home to dust, dark and the occasional spider, the space underneath a child's can be a mysterious landscape. And, in the active imagination of a child, it's the perfect place for nightmarish monsters to dwell. Thankfully, not *all* of these creatures have a hankering for eating children. Many are happy enough to settle for making friends and acting as a fur coat. This may found far-fetched, but it's a very real scenario and one that's experienced by *Chris and Crumble.*

Life for Chris is simple enough in her semi-detached house. She leads an uncomplicated life of drinking tea, going to the seaside and attending flower shows. Most importantly all her clothes are free of chew marks. Nonetheless, things are about to change with the emergence of Crumble from under her bed. Far from a salivating, flesh eating monster, Crumble is more of a pink, cuddly mop head with two furry legs.

Although her gender is never directly referred to, Crumble is obviously female due to her fluttering eyelashes. And, if you want further proof, she gives birth to eight baby 'crumbles' partway through the series. These crumbles are a friendly bunch, but their penchant for a fabric based diet does tend to decimate the contents of Chris' wardrobe. Chris copes admirably with the loss of her clothes and tries to continue her existence as normal. In spite of these efforts, life is never normal with Crumble and her offspring around.

The crumbles energetic digging at the beach leaves Chris stranded in a sand trap as the tide comes in. Whilst being displayed as Crumbalia Exotica at a flower show, the crumbles develop a strong desire to eat a judge's cardigan. And Chris learns the hard way that you should never give Crumble a cup of tea. And you certainly shouldn't try and dry her out next to a fire.

You could be forgiven for having never heard of *Chris and Crumble*. It was a series whose tenure in the schedules was brief and, despite a repeat airing in 1990, has subsequently slid into obscurity. Despite *Chris and Crumble's* legacy lacking gravitas, it's notable for being one of the final shows produced for the BBC's See-Saw slot. Seven 10-minute episodes emerged from the BBC2 schedules with these mini-narratives going out at 1.30pm on Mondays. The show was overseen by producer Maurice Pooley with animator Tom Bailey providing the stories and pictures.

But what was it like? Well, visually it's very cute. Chris has a mop of thick, brown hair aligned with big rosy cheeks while Crumble exudes a loveable, cuddly charm in the same way that Labrador puppies do. There's a definite 1970s influence to the visual aesthetic and the soundtrack, with its jaunty synths, is also deliciously retro and dreamlike. Despite these nostalgic shades, the series eschews any cultural references to retain a timeless look.

Equally ageless is Peter Hawkins' narration. One of the less discussed stars of children's TV, Hawkins' CV is incredible. His body of work includes voice work on the *Flower Pot Men, Rainbow* (as the original Zippy), *Captain Pugwash* and *SuperTed*. While his voice leans towards an authoritative tone, it's one which is coated in geniality. And it perfectly matches the narratives of *Chris and Crumble*.

There's no need to indulge heavily in the jeopardy stakes when it comes to the under-fives; *Chris and Crumble* sticks to this advice. Trips to a jumble sale and the beach are never going to get the pulse racing. In the eyes of a young child, however, these locations are astonishing, marvel-filled paradises. The narratives may not stick in the mind for long afterwards, but they're fun little romps. So, while *Chris and Crumble* is unlikely to ever be offered up as a shining example of its genre, it can tick off some of the most essential boxes.

THE BUBBLEGUM BRIGADE

ITV
1989

No one is immune from a broken heart. Anyone on the age spectrum from one to one hundred can be afflicted. Often, for a one year old, this heartbreak comes from not being allowed to watch what they want on television. And, within 10 minutes, this turmoil is over. But the emotional impact is still a harrowing experience. Thankfully, as you mature, you begin to form a perspective on what constitutes a broken heart. Dealing with them, though, remains a hardship. So, wouldn't it be fantastic if there was an organisation dedicated to mending broken hearts? Well there is. It's *The Bubblegum Brigade.*

William (Bill Oddie) is the leader of The Bubblegum Brigade, an organisation licensed to mend broken hearts while you wait. Broken hearts are tough assignments to tackle, so William needs a great deal of help. And this assistance comes courtesy of his family. Joining their father as members of The Bubblegum Brigade are Alph (Ian Kirkby), Bunny (Michelle Moore), Fuddle (James Hyden) and Jinx (Flora Fenton). Located on the periphery of this family unit is the domineering figure of Auntie Doodah (Veronica Clifford) and wacky super computer Walli (Masquerade).

And The Bubblegum Brigade need to deal with a wide range of broken hearts. A legion of distraught pop music fans get in touch after hot new pop trio The Three B's cancel a concert. A young girl's happiness is threatened when she has to celebrate her birthday without any friends or family. And a German

Shepherd seeks help when he discovers that his favourite tree is about to be chopped down by the council.

The Bubblegum Brigade started life not as a series in its own right, but as a one-off instalment of the *Dramarama* anthology series in 1988. Following the commission of a full series, Bill Oddie and Laura Beaumont began writing *The Bubblegum Brigade* with six episodes arriving on ITV in 1989. The programme rose, as Oddie recalls, from the ashes of an earlier show – *From the Top* – that the couple had written:

"We loved doing From the Top, but then they ran out of money. Nearly. However, they seemed anxious for us to produce something else. And it was called The Bubblegum Brigade. I have no idea who thought of that title, but it wasn't us. In fact we were sort of embarrassed by it. We hated it. However one of the cardinal lessons of TV is: if you're offered a series, take it! Even if only the producer likes the title. We were also guided towards what it was about: Bunch of kids, various ages and one or two adults, especially me! What did they do? They solve people's problems, no matter how silly. Sounds like the Goodies! Oh and there's a robot in it! Sounds like Metal Mickey!"

Writing with his spouse was, as Oddie recalls, no different to working with anyone else, although external forces did bring unwanted problems:

"Graeme Garden and I wrote The Goodies both apart and together. Half each. Then we joined them together. We very rarely workshopped or improvised. We challenged people to spot the join! Laura and I worked that way. No doubt some people suspected family nepotism, but, in fact, she wrote more than I did and I was happy to let her! However she – and we –

got weary of the production team asking ME the questions. My frequent reply was truthfully 'Laura wrote that one, any questions ask her. I didn't have anything to do with that one.' We were both resentful of this. Laura vowed that, no disrespect, but from then on we would not write together. And we haven't. She continues to work in TV comedy, especially animation. I switched to bird watching"

Although *The Bubblegum Brigade* shares an agency setting with *The Goodies* (and Bill Oddie's presence) this is where the similarities end. The Goodies tackled anything, but The Bubblegum Brigade's focus is on broken hearts. It's a serviceable premise which allows plenty of emotion and tension to come through the agency doors.

And it's wedded to a gleeful silliness which embraces visual comedy. Alph and William update the Trojan Horse trope by smuggling themselves into a boy band's mansion within a giant cake. On the trail of a distraught dog, The Bubblegum Brigade mimic its every action, even stealing sausages from a butcher. And there's even time for a magnificent meta-joke where William rings his 'brother' Bill for some ornithological advice.

Oddie is clearly the star amongst the cast. And, with 25 years' experience in television comedy at this point, his mastery of the form is assured. Oddie's brand of comedy is one that scoffs at the mere idea of slotting into a narrow demographic. It's playful, it's intelligent and it's quintessentially British. He can tickle funny bones regardless of age, a rare talent and one that British television should be proud of.

Therefore, Oddie is the perfect fit for a children's show. And he slots seamlessly into *The Bubblegum Brigade* whilst maintaining a fine chemistry with his young co-stars. And, as he is keen to state, working with a young cast is a proposition that he rarely passes on:

"Both Laura and I enjoy working with youngsters. The theatrical gene means they are anxious to please and don't misbehave. Much. It is also often easier to work on routines or scenes with the younger generation. I think it helps that both Laura and I have had careers in music and comedy. We are as they say up to speed with the young folk"

The young cast populating *The Bubblegum Brigade* are a lively, enthusiastic bunch, but only one of them went on to pursue acting as a career. Several years (and many inches) above the rest of his siblings in *The Bubblegum Brigade,* Ian Kirkby exhibits a precocious talent for comedy. A product of the Central Junior Television Workshop, Kirkby had previously appeared in *Your Mother Wouldn't Like It* and this shows in his excellent comic timing.

Oddie can't remember any discussion regarding a second series and perhaps one was enough. However, despite its brief tenure on our screens, *The Bubblegum Brigade* is worthy of discussion. We're all aware of Oddie's talents, but Laura Beaumont's are given the chance to shine here. The scripts are lively, fun and, most importantly, gloriously silly. And that's one of the most crucial combinations as far as children's television is concerned. So, let's take *The Bubblegum Brigade* down from that dusty ledge in our memory, give it a polish and remember it as a wholesome show full of giggles.

JELLYNECK

ITV
1989

Life can take us on many twists and turns, yet as we get older we learn how to manoeuvre our way through it a little better. At least that's what we tell ourselves. Sure, we develop the skills for dealing with intrusive relatives turning up unannounced at weekends. But do we ever get to grips with supermarkets relocating products from one aisle to another?

We should, really, count ourselves lucky. Even our most bizarre trials and tribulations take place within the realms of reality. And these boundaries, mundane though they are, protect us from most of the madness our imaginations can summon up. However, imagine a world where there are no boundaries to creativity. That world is *Jellyneck*.

Albert Albert (Chris England) is a man for all seasons. But in the universe of *Jellyneck* the seasons are as unpredictable as anything he's seen before. Albert, of course, doesn't *want* to venture into this unusual world. But he always ends up there through no fault of his own. One moment he can be in his kitchen putting on a jumper, but when he emerges from his woolly cladding he can find himself outside a country house. Likewise, Albert can be rummaging in his attic for antiques when, upon banging his head on a beam, he is transported into a tree in a middle of a field. And the tree wants to eat him.

It's a curious world to say the least. And we haven't even started discussing the inhabitants of this alternate dimension. Fitter's Mate (Morwenna Banks) is the most regular thorn in

Albert's side and it's a thorn which is particularly ugly, revolting and stupid. Fitter's Mate is so called as he's the mate of Fitter (Andy Taylor), a carpet fitter who, in his long and distinguished career, has fitted zero carpets.

Albert also encounters Slapper (Andy Taylor) and Slaphead (Chris Lang) on a number of occasions. These two chaps do exactly what their names indicate, so you can expect to find Slapper regularly slapping Slaphead on his bald bonce. All of these characters are relatively normal compared to Silas Bogg (Andy Taylor). A giant of a man, Silas Bogg is coloured entirely blue and has a habit of shrinking once bitten on the bottom.

It's amongst these odd fellows, and many others, that Albert finds himself on a series of adventures. Albert's adventures may, on face value, appear rather mundane. Delivering a tray of onions to Silas Bogg, for example, isn't exactly a scintillating premise. But these are no ordinary onions. These are onions that come to life and cause Albert moral headaches.

Other episodes are outrageous concepts from the get go. And this is why Albert, in the company of explorer Count Vasco, discovers a coastline in his bathroom which leads to a new continent and the theft of Albert's umbrella. Albert also encounters a four-armed businesswoman and the 'kitchen of doom' whilst he's on the hunt for Guffard Giggler, a custard obsessed idiot.

Jellyneck was developed by producer Debbie Gates and was the final member in a quartet of shows dedicated to storytelling. *Tales from Fat Tulip's Garden* with Tony Robinson had aired in 1985 on ITV. Ben Keaton then took over the performing duties with 1988's *Gumtree* on Channel 4 in 1988. And, around the same time that *Gumtree* was airing, *Revolting Animals* was debuting over on ITV.

Revolting Animals was notable in that it was the first of Gates' imaginative programmes to feature more than one performer. And it was this same team of performers which went on to make up the cast of *Jellyneck*. Chris England discusses the beginnings of *Jellyneck*:

"Debbie Gates had success with a show called Fat Tulip, in which Tony Robinson acted out these strange stories while he was telling them. Revolting Animals was her way of developing this style for pairs of comic performers who could play off each other. Morwenna Banks and I did four of the stories, Chris Lang and Andy Taylor also did four.

We kind of knew each other already, I think, from doing comedy shows at the Edinburgh Festival – they were a sketch trio called The Jockeys of Norfolk (along with a fellow called Hugh Grant, not sure what became of him), and Morwenna and I did a show called The Preventers, a spoof of classic sixties adventure with our friend Robert Harley (one of the brains behind the very successful Green Wing).

After Revolting Animals, Debbie reckoned the next logical step was to develop her storytelling approach into a group thing, aimed at older children than her previous projects, which would enable all sorts of fun and games, slapstick, rudeness, multiple crazy characters and situations. So she bunged the four of us together and told us to come up with something. It was great, the sort of thing that hardly ever happens"

As with *Fat Tulip's Garden* and *Revolting Animals,* Central Television produced *Jellyneck* for Children's ITV with the six episodes airing at 4.20pm on Wednesday afternoons. Unlike the previous takes on storytelling, which were filmed in and around London, *Jellyneck* returned to Central's spiritual home of

Birmingham for filming. It was, as Chris England recounts, a magnificent experience for all involved in the production:

"We filmed it in the countryside around Birmingham, in and around the most odd-looking buildings they could find, follies and the like. The quality of the filming made it look a different beast to the other children's television at the time, which was very studio-based and on video. I think it made the crazy stories really stand out. And it felt like we were working on little movies, which was a treat.

The main challenge I remember was that director Jeremy McCracken wanted everything indoors to be softened by vast quantities of smoke, to show up beams of light, and make everything seem a bit other-worldly. So there were these incense burners going the whole time, and by the end of the day this black muck had crept into every pore, eyes, nose, mouth, ears, fingernails. A small thing, though. I remember it as a very happy time"

If you've previously encountered a show with Debbie Gates at the helm then you should know what to expect with *Jellyneck*. While *Jackanory* may be more iconic, it can't hold a candle to the level of invention and irreverence she deploys with the art of storytelling. Children are a pure distillation of manic chaos and Gates' understanding of this is hardwired into all her productions. *Jellyneck* doesn't shy away from this approach and, as Chris England highlights, this is down to Gates' influence:

"Debbie was tremendously positive, and her enthusiasm for her projects spread through the whole production team. She was always very supportive of even the craziest ideas, because she always wanted to see what was going to happen next. And that's how come we got away with Slapper and Slaphead, and a character who makes farting noises in a bowl of custard,

163

and the earwax collector, and all sorts of mad stuff. And she really went to bat for Jellyneck at ITV, and got us a second series, but sadly her health deteriorated and it never came to fruition"

The stories within *Jellyneck* may contain standard three act narratives, but that's where any sense of familiarity ends. You will not have heard stories like these before. They are absurd and brimming with an infectiously surreal energy. There's a Monty Python and Goodies-like zeal to the episodes where anything and everything can happen.

Polo players run around with their horses on their back. Fitter's Mate desperately tries to chat up a painting which comes to life. And a tool library attempts to enforce a strict 8-second loan policy. These absurd shades help to colour an outrageous world where everyman Albert Albert is stranded as a lone voice of reason. His is a mission to succeed against the odds, no matter how ridiculous they are, and he does so with an unwavering determination.

Bringing these stories to life are the magnificent performances. There's a seamless interchange between the performers with a remarkably fast paced dialogue. The chemistry on offer is top drawer and you can see how this has been bolstered by the team's previous work together.

And the characters that they inhabit are a sheer delight. Andy Taylor and Chris Lang have a ball with an array of grotesque creations such as the shrieking Redface and Adrian Vickers, a man obsessed with collecting the black bits from under his toenails. Perhaps the vilest creation is reserved for Morwenna Banks with Fitter's Mate, a character that she elevates to hitherto unknown levels of irritation.

164

The beauty of these performances is that they take place with a minimum of props and, in lieu of this, rely on the viewer's imagination. It's a common theme of Debbie Gates' work and, in *Jellyneck,* it's pushed to a new extreme as a result of the multiple performances.

Jellyneck brings a new strain of vibrancy to Gates' menagerie of storytelling and it's strange that it's not more feted in the history books. A second series may have helped to strengthen its legacy, but sadly this was not to be. Still, one run of brilliance is a fantastic return. And those who embraced its peculiar methods will never forget it.

PIGSTY

BBC1
1990 – 1991

Pigs are a curious species. With their snuffling noses, mud covered backs and rotund bodies, they're hardly the epitome of attractiveness. But people LOVE pigs. And this is perhaps why they feature so frequently in our fiction. The Three Little Pigs, Miss Piggy and Napoleon from Animal Farm are just a few of the porcine protagonists to litter our consciousness. But what about the porky gang of Troyboy, Pinks and Little Pig? Are they guilty of cluttering up our memory banks? Well, no, not really. So, let's head over to *Pigsty,* grab a milkshake and see what we can remember.

Promo Park is the hottest recording studio in the country. All the biggest pop stars want to cut their next big hit in this sprawling complex. And this is despite the chaotic efforts of complex manager Martin Trotter (Mark Hadfield), better known as MT. An overambitious man, MT yearns to be a successful businessman. Unfortunately he's more bumbling idiot than high flyer. However, if he fancies a break from bumbling, he can always head down to the Pigsty for a bite to eat. After all, what could go wrong in a fast food restaurant?

An establishment unlike no other, the Pigsty is an American styled fast food restaurant housed within Promo Park. And it's staffed entirely by pigs. Yes, actual pigs. Troyboy (Richard Gauntlett) and Pinks (Tessa Crockett) are a pair of American siblings with a passion for making fast food. They're joined by their young British cousin Little Pig (Peter Mandell) to

166

complete a piggy triumvirate. When this trio aren't rummaging through the Pigsty bins they're banging heads with MT.

And these tensions power a succession of comedic narratives. Chaos ensues when a planned visit from the sanitary inspector coincides with a dog on the loose in Promo Park. The pigs come to loggerheads with MT when he decides they need a personal trainer. And Little Pig's pet rat escapes on the very same day that Princess Sophie of San Marino pays a visit.

Pigs may be, rather unfairly, labelled as being lazy, but there was nothing slack behind the production of *Pigsty*. The 18 episodes, which aired across two series in 10-minute instalments, were all written by Paul Mendelson and produced by Pippa Dyson. It was with BBC1's *May to December* that, a year before *Pigsty,* that Mendelson had first tasted success with his scripts. As well as several more series of *May to December*, he would also go on to pen the sitcoms *So Haunt Me* and *My Hero*. Mendelson recalls his early steps into *Pigsty:*

"As I can recall Pippa Dyson approached my then agent Ian Amos at ICM. She was delightful. Really friendly and professional. We got on very well. Pippa had clearly seen something in my writing that she liked and she told me she hadn't wanted a children's writer − rather a comedy writer who wrote about amiable people, who wrote clean but funny, wasn't afraid of emotion and wouldn't talk down to kids. And she felt I had a good visual sense, which of course coming from an advertising background as I did was a prerequisite. I also had young kids of my own, which helped"

Both series of *Pigsty* received repeats in the Children's BBC schedule, yet memories of the programme remain scarce. The main overriding memory, for those who remember the show, is

167

of one specific element: the pig masks. And these memories tend to be lodged in nightmare territory. However, *are* they scary? Well, you certainly wouldn't want to see one peering through your bedroom window at night, but they're no more terrifying than the contents of MT's wardrobe.

The pig masks may not be scary, but they still provide a visual hook for the series. And it helps *Pigsty* stand out from anything else in its genre. You *could* argue that the whole pig angle isn't necessary. And that humans could easily staff the Pigsty. Doesn't sound very fun, though, does it? Pigs are inherently funnier. Paul Mendelson is aware of this potential and infuses this into the comedic setup of *Pigsty*.

Mendelson's CV shows the fact that he's a man who knows how to write a sitcom. And *Pigsty* underlines this fact in bold. The episodes are peppered with a wealth of piggy gags such as rummaging through the bins for rotten food, but there's also the comic brilliance of MT. A man whose petard is frequently hoisted, MT's greed and ambition drives the episodes with lashings of comedy.

Mark Hadfield may be better known for his work on the stage, yet he's equally at home on the small screen and has been popping up since the early 1990s. He captures the arrogance of MT with a real élan and then punctures this by revealing the character to be little more than a flailing, wet lettuce.

The actors behind the pig masks may not have had the career as Hadfield, but this is by no means a barometer of their talent. Richard Gauntlett projects Troyboy's good time confidence with an effortless sheen. Tessa Crockett harnesses a brash American accent to infuse Pinks with authority. And Peter Mandell's devil-may-care attitude chimes perfectly with

168

the young viewers.

The cast also have a superb dynamic at play. One episode can find them frantically trying to hide a semi-naked MT from Princess Sophia. Another may involve taking on the manic whirlwind that is music manager Mr Little (he's huge). Whatever the predicament there's a strong chemistry between the cast which holds the plots together.

It all combines to produce a fantastic little sitcom for the under 10s. And it's clever too. Businessmen and pop stars are routinely parodied. Characters break the fourth wall. And multiple plots are all resolved within 10 minutes. *Pigsty* isn't as well remembered as ITV's vaguely similar *Spatz* (albeit without pigs) but it deserves a little more appreciation.

THE SUPER MARIO CHALLENGE

The Children's Channel
1991

If you ventured into any branch of Dixons on a Saturday morning in the early 1990s then you were guaranteed to see one thing: a bunch of children. And these children were ecstatic. Crowded round a rather battered looking NES, they were having their minds blown by the infectious playability of Super Mario Bros.

This Mario mania would soon spread far beyond Dixons. Aside from the games there was also the merchandise. Lots of merchandise. British television quickly picked up on this obsession with Italian plumbers and button bashing. And, loading up a brief burst of teatime excitement, *The Super Mario Challenge* was born.

The Super Mario Challenge is out to find the best Super Mario player in the universe. It's a bold quest. And one that host John Lenahan (dressed in Mario overalls) is determined to complete. The simplest way to discover this champion of champions is to play Super Mario. Head to head. In front of an audience of blocks, pipes and screaming children.

Throughout a sequence of heats, the young contestants battle against each other whilst playing the first three Super Mario Bros. games. Episodes contain three rounds which include a speed challenge, a coin collect round and, finally, a points round. Coins are awarded to the winner of each round and the contestant with the most at the end advances into the next stage of the competition. Awaiting the overall winner of the competition is not only the crown of best Super Mario player in the universe, but also a family holiday to Denmark.

Gaming was a virtually unknown television format in 1991. The Children's Channel was about to change that. Predating the genre-defining *Games Master* by a year, *The Super Mario Challenge* debuted in September and ran daily until December. The majority of these ten minute episodes were dedicated to the knockout competition, although the series was also punctuated with celebrity specials. These editions featured guests such as Tessa Sanderson, Keith Chegwin, Chris Evans and Keith Harris going head to head.

John Lenahan's most notable role on British television is as the Talkie Toaster in Red Dwarf, but his main profession has always been magic. *The Super Mario Challenge*, though, would be a very different proposition to anything he had previously done. Lenahan recalls the audition being relatively straightforward

"It was an open audition. Someone at my agent's office jokingly said 'With your moustache you should go up for this' and I thought it was a good idea. I had a pair of overalls and I put them on. It is very rare for me to audition and usually they are disasters but this one was great. I remember, after the meeting, saying to my agent: I got this job"

However, when it came to recording the series, Lenaham remembers it being a tough gig:

"It was made on the cheap and one of the hardest things I have ever done. We did a pilot over one weekend, but when it came to the series we recorded 15 shows a day! I often wondered if that was a record. By the end

171

of the day I was babbling so much I used to ask the director to keep an ear on me, to make sure I was still making sense. It was a really hard shoot. The cameras were disguised as mushrooms which meant the red lights were covered – so I never knew what camera was on me. I also had an earpiece but they were unable to isolate it, so I not only got my direction but I also had all of the cameras' direction in my ear the whole time"

Consoles are now a firm fixture in British homes, but at the start of the 1990s they held a more limited presence. Most children had to make do with playing on a Spectrum, Commodore 64 or an Amstrad for their gaming pleasures. And this involved a lengthy load time. Seeing a NES in action, therefore, was very exciting. *The Super Mario Challenge* captures this excitement and distils it into its purest form: head to head challenges which are almost over in the blink of an eye. John Lenahan needs little time to explain each round before the contestants are jumping on Koopa Troopas.

Lenahan makes for a worthy host and, without stopping to take a breath, conveys an almost continuous stream of commentary during the rounds. Having been an Atari ST gamer some years previously, Lenahan wasn't overly familiar with the NES. A crash course in Mario was needed. Despite his wife's protestations, he locked himself away for five hours a day to play Super Mario games.

And his research pays off. He knows the Mario universe inside out and couples this with an engaging personality to get the kids on his side. Lenahan's showmanship really comes to the fore during the celebrity specials. The repartee and crosstalk flows with a more anarchic edge and Lenahan recalls being carried out of the studio by Janice Long and Chris Evans.

The series, made in association with Nintendo, is clearly a promotional push for the NES and, in particular, Super Mario Bros. 3, but this is far from an infomercial. Nintendo's involvement is minimal and the main focus is on children playing games. And, at 10 minutes long, the episodes are the right length to maintain the attention. Any longer and the Mario novelty would have started to wear thin.

As a one-off *The Super Mario Challenge* works very well, but one series was probably enough. A little more variety would be required to engage a viewer over a longer running time and that's what *Games Master* would achieve a year later. Even so, *The Super Mario Challenge* got the ball rolling and deserves credit for establishing the competitive element.

WYSIWYG

ITV
1992

The days of having to cope with just two, three or four television channels are long, long gone. As a result of advances in cable TV, satellite television and the internet, our televisual landscape has changed beyond all recognition. Hundreds of different channels from all around the world are now available to be beamed directly into our front rooms.

It doesn't guarantee higher levels of quality, but at least the option is there to watch ancient episodes of *Bullseye*. However, this choice and availability stops at the edges of our planet's atmosphere. And, in the grand scheme of the infinite universe, this means we're missing out on a lot of alien television channels. Thankfully, to give us a taster, a special introductory offer is on its way thanks to *Wysiwyg*.

Intergalactic TV (IGTV) is the proud broadcaster of what it claims is the very best television from around the galaxy. And Earth, or Flurt's Globe as it's known to non-Earthlings, is about to receive some trial broadcasts of IGTV. The most prominent programme on offer in these trial broadcasts centres around Wysiwyg (Nick Wilton).

With his trusty ear plug in place, which contains all Earth knowledge, Wysiwyg presents a number of documentaries about life on Earth. These programmes are recorded by the hovering, orb known as Rovercam. And, when it comes to all technical matters, the simple and content Globule (Clive Mantle) is on hand to take care of these.

174

Wysiwyg's broadcasts, along with the rest of IGTV's trial, are not the result of consensual decisions from the people of Earth. Rather than politely slotting into an allocated channel, IGTV forces its schedule into the existing schedules. Earth based shows such as quiz show Joke Busters, Australian soap Round These Parts and cowboy movie Apache Bottom are all rudely interrupted by the IGTV signal.

And what exactly does IGTV have to offer? First and foremost it's Wysiwyg and his documentaries. These cover such diverse human affairs as shopping, fashion and teachers. The results are disastrous and ham-fisted affairs, but Wysiwyg refuses to accept defeat and stumbles proudly on to the end. In between Wysiwyg's clumsy reporting, IGTV provides a number of other programmes to excite the senses. These shows, and Wysiwyg's segments, are linked to by the digital, red face of Mer-dokk (Julie Dawn Cole), an emotionless in-vision continuity announcer.

Tantalizing glimpses of IGTV's programming include hilarious home video show Galactic Gloopers, history is tackled by How They are Then and situation comedy is taken care of by Are You Being Varped? In between the programmes there's plenty of time for advertising with products such as Bot Extench and Niffnibblers being hawked to viewers. *Wysiwyg* completes its content with an assortment of ridiculously inane dialogues between Shaz (Linda Hartley-Clarke) and Maz (Julie Dawn Cole)

Wysiwyg was produced by Yorkshire Television with Patrick Titley in the dual role as producer and director. Only five episodes were produced with these 25-minute bursts of comedy airing on Mondays at 4.15pm. Yet the laughs, as Nick Wilton

175

reveals, were not so prevalent behind the scenes of *Wysiwyg:*

> *"I was approached to come up with an idea for a series by the producer who I'd worked with on episodes of The Book Tower and Microlive. It was meant for older kids up to 9-11 years old, but CITV put it out too early so it was never seen by its proper target audience. I then had a big argument on the rights (after it went out) which I (sort of) won. I ended up getting 50% of the rights, even though nearly all of it was my idea with some input from the producer. Unfortunately, it was a pyrrhic victory as my owning 50% meant it was never repeated!"*

Wysiwyg is, for all intents and purposes, a sketch show. But, although the standard sketch show format is serviceable enough, *Wysiwyg* is a little cleverer. Rather than banging out sketch after sketch the show installs a framework based around IGTV. The result is an immediate identity and a universe with a set of rules and a clear theme.

At the forefront of this world is Wysiwyg, a character in the time honoured tradition of the fool. Wysiwyg is determined to be successful and professional, but he constantly makes a rod for his own back. His pompous, misplaced confidence provides an eternal thorn in his side. And that's what comedy is all about. He's well-meaning, of course, and coupled with Globule's obliviousness, Wysiwyg's segments have a gentle charm which never leave your heckles reaching skywards.

The comedy present within *Wysiwyg* is strong and when you take a look at the writing credits you can see why. Peter Baynham and Ben Miller, both in the early stages of their careers and pals of Wilton, are on hand to provide evidence of their burgeoning quality. Laura Beaumont, a regular contributor to children's television, also pops up in the credits to cement the quality. Along with Nick Wilton, who was involved in almost every aspect of the production, this writing team serve up a wide range of comedic styles.

The most prominent area of comedy explored is the parody. Australian soap Round These Parts makes light of the high drama built up around everyday life and Kidd's Klubb is Timmy Mallett turned up to 11. There are also some superb standalone sketches. One sketch finds a customer going in to a shop that sells nothing in particular and is packed to the brim with nothing. Another sketch focuses on a man who has leapt onto a train head to Edinburgh at Doncaster (even though the train didn't stop there) and wants to go to Brighton.

Quite why *Wysiwyg* remains shrouded in obscurity is a puzzling circumstance. The performances throughout the show are of a high calibre, the scripts bubble along with a comedic effervescence and they contain a wonderful stream of surreal flourishes. Best of all, there's a glorious cameo from Bob Holness in full *Blockbusters* mode. There's more than enough on offer to warrant a second series (or, at the least, a sixth episode). Sadly this never materialised. In spite of that, *Wysiwyg* remains an obscurity that holds its own in the arena of children's television.

Acknowledgements

Roger Stevenson
Joy Whitby
Tim Brooke-Taylor
Peter Charlton
Derek Griffiths
Fred Harris
Freddie Davies
Kathy Jones
Greg Knowles
Kirsty Miller
Wingham Rowan
Robin Lyons
Paul Greenwood
Nick Wilton
Avril Rowlands
Rick Vanes
Patricia Pearson
Matilda Thorpe
Gareth Jones
Tony Sands
Jenny Kenna
Bill Oddie
Chris England
Paul Mendelson
John Lenahan
Christian Swain
Nathan Pattinson
Ben Morton
The BFI Archive
Simon Goretzki